'In *The Tyranny of Identity* Professor Pietroni once again demonstrates he is always the scholar, always the professor, always the teacher, and always the intellectual guide. In this most readable and understandable work he guides the reader through his own search for identity and helps the reader to understand the most human of questions, "*What is the current state of the world, and what is my role within that world?*" The work is brilliant, immensely readable, insightful, and reflective for both the author and the reader. Professor Pietroni is one of the world's leading compassion scholars and he demonstrates his compassion for others as well as for himself.'

John-Robert Curtin, PhD, professor, author and poet.

'Professor Pietroni's reflections on his experience of "otherness" are shared with honesty and vulnerability, revealing a multi-faceted identity, and an enriched personal, professional, and cultural life. This book is a much-needed call for compassion and humanity in our troubled world.'

Dr Kathryn Waddington, Emerita Fellow in Psychology, University of Westminster, UK.

The Tyranny of Identity

The Tyranny of Identity is both a personal and highly interdisciplinary examination of the wide range of factors and disciplines at play in the formation of identity. It takes a novel and unique approach to this through use of metaphor, images, poetry and a wide range of academic sources to provide a holistic approach to the study of identity.

This book uses the concept of Babushka dolls to show that we all have a series of activities during our lives that reside in our mind, body, spirit – each influencing the multiple identities we knowingly or unknowingly possess. This collage of factors and forces allows us to create an identity. The layers of identity unfold as the chapters progress and in doing so the book addresses the manifold ways in which identity intersects with nationhood, politics, education, the culture wars, family, religion, gender and contemporary institutions.

The Tyranny of Identity is a wide-ranging, cross-cultural book that integrates and explores how the issue of identity has become a central issue in every academic discipline. This book is essential reading to all students studying identity and all readers seeking a deeper understanding of this complex topic.

Professor Pietroni, DSc (Hon), FRCP, FRCGP, MFPH, is former Dean of General Practice at the London University. He currently lives in Shrewsbury, Shropshire, UK, which is the place of Charles Darwin's birth.

He is the author of several books, including, *The Greening of Medicine, Holistic Living, The Poetry of Compassion* and *Innovation in Community Care and Primary Health: The Marylebone Experiment*. Professor Pietroni has taught at six universities in the USA.

The Tyranny of Identity

Professor Pietroni

LONDON AND NEW YORK

Designed cover image: © Getty Images

First published 2024
by Routledge
4 Park Square, Milton Park, Abingdon, Oxon OX14 4RN

and by Routledge
605 Third Avenue, New York, NY 10158

Routledge is an imprint of the Taylor & Francis Group, an informa business

© 2024 Patrick Pietroni

The right of Patrick Pietroni to be identified as author of this work has been asserted in accordance with sections 77 and 78 of the Copyright, Designs and Patents Act 1988.

All rights reserved. No part of this book may be reprinted or reproduced or utilised in any form or by any electronic, mechanical, or other means, now known or hereafter invented, including photocopying and recording, or in any information storage or retrieval system, without permission in writing from the publishers.

Trademark notice: Product or corporate names may be trademarks or registered trademarks, and are used only for identification and explanation without intent to infringe.

British Library Cataloguing-in-Publication Data
A catalogue record for this book is available from the British Library

ISBN: 978-1-032-51264-8 (hbk)
ISBN: 978-1-032-51263-1 (pbk)
ISBN: 978-1-003-40141-4 (ebk)

DOI: 10.4324/9781003401414

Typeset in Times New Roman
by Apex CoVantage, LLC

**Dedicated to Marilyn Miller,
who helped me find my voice
and
Acknowledgements too many to list,
but without Lee Good this book would
never have been written.**

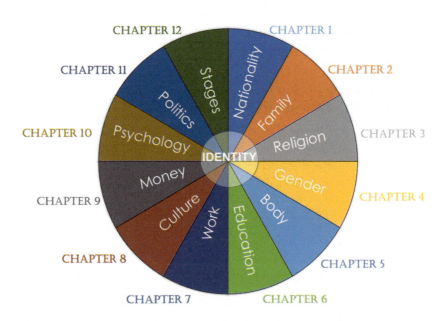

Figure 0FM.1

Contents

	Introduction	1
1	Nationality, Race, Tribes, Caste	5
2	Family, Social	19
3	Religion, Beliefs	33
4	Gender, Gender Role, Genetics	47
5	The Body, Body Type, Body Image	61
6	Education, Training, Learning	71
7	Work, Professional Positions	85
8	Culture, Culture Wars	115
9	Money, Wealth, Status	123
10	Psychology, Psychiatry, Psychoanalysis	133
11	Politics, Philosophy	151
12	The Stages, the Seasons and the Life-Cycle of Man's Life	169
	Index	*194*

Introduction

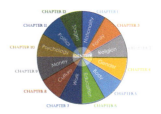

Figure 0.0

The issue of "identity" has received an ever increasing scholarly and political attention in the last decade. Whether it is the issue of race that we continue to return to or the focus on gender and concern regarding reconstructive surgery the debate still centres on the issue of identity. Is identity determined by our genes, or linked to the nation we were born in, what it says on our passport – Citizen of x? Or is identity shaped by our character and personality, or is it what we feel about ourselves – "our sense of self"? The list that one can construct to try and interrogate the word *identity* and its meaning is long and continues to increase. The issues of unconscious bias, privileged ignorance, moral tribes, religious faiths, culture wars, are only some of additional subjects that impinge and impact on the concept of identity. I provide an extensive map at the end of this introduction which is followed by a more detailed exploration chapter by chapter with a "shortish" book list after each.

However, the main purpose and drive in my deciding to address this huge subject (knowing that it would require many libraries to include and address what is available on the subject) is to erase from our debates the necessity of believing we have one identity only.

There is too much of who we are, who we have been and who we can become to include in this one word *identity*. I had thoughts of entitling the book either:

The Tyranny of One Identity
or
The Freedom of Identities

You may or may not agree with me after finishing this book. I, however, hope to convince otherwise, for in my own search for my identity I discovered and came to accept my many identities.

An image I have found helpful is that of the classical Russian doll. These were known as Matryoshka dolls, or Babushka dolls. They consist of a series of wooden dolls each in decreasing size that are placed one by one in each other. They commonly are designed to designate different themes (fairy tale characters,

DOI: 10.4324/9781003401414-1

2 Introduction

Figure 0.1 Babushka Dolls

political leaders). The largest set made included 51 separate dolls. I use Matryoshka dolls as a metaphor for our different identities that we have possessed throughout our lives and how, whether we acknowledge them or not, they reside in us and will and do influence who we are and who we become.

My own Babushka doll includes the twelve "dolls" I use to outline how complex the issue of identity is and how narrow and incorrect the belief that we have only one identity is.

Each chapter expands and explores the 12 different aspects of identity I have personally explored searching for my own identity. I start each chapter with a short biographical section describing my own journey and how my own "doll" has impacted on the identities I have collected. The second section interrogates the academic literature written concerning the theme. In the third section I try to comment on my own current understanding of how I have been influenced by this "doll" over the years.

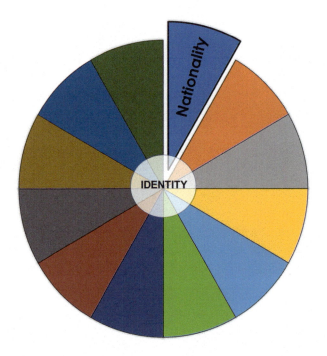

Figure 1.0

1 Nationality, Race, Tribes, Caste

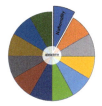

Figure 1.0

Section 1: Biography

I was born in Cyprus (1942), a small island in the Eastern Mediterranean. The third son in a family of four boys. My four grandparents were of different nationalities; on my mother's side my grandparents were of French and Italian origin, on my father's side they were Greek and from Anatolia. My ancestor, born between 1850–1860 in Anatolia, came to Cyprus when he was two and married a Spanish lady, Theophilla Rose. There are different versions of the name Pietroni, some romantic and almost certainly false. Joseph Pietroni, my great-great-grandfather, was a highway bandit. Pursued by the police, he took refuge in the Roman Catholic Church and changed his name from Josephides (Son of Joseph). Because he was Catholic he favoured the Western tradition of a lasting surname, rather than taking the name of his father i.e. he was not only a "bandit", he was also a snob! He chose Pietroni believing it was the original name.

What links the disparate parts of my ancestry were the French language, the Roman Catholic Church (my uncle became the Pope's representative in Cyprus) and a very firm link and loyalty to the British Colonial culture. Like Amin Maalouf[1] in his book on identity, I will start with the issue of national identity and then outline briefly my own pursuit of how my search for identity developed.

Cyprus and a Brief Historical Background

Any and every Empire that considered themselves Great has invaded, conquered and possessed Cyprus over at least the past 3,000 years. Phoenicians, Egyptians, Ancient Greece, the Roman Empire, Crusaders (both English and French), Turkey (Ottoman Empire). The second British Occupation occurred after the Congress of Berlin in 1878 in the Treaty of San Stefano. In the *Convention of Defensive Alliance*, the Sultan Abdul Hamid II undertook to assign the island of Cyprus to be *occupied and administered by England*.[2] The purpose of this treaty was to enable Great Britain to fulfil her support to the Sultan against Russian aggression. At the end of the First World War when Turkey chose the wrong side, Britain annexed

DOI: 10.4324/9781003401414-2

6 Nationality, Race, Tribes, Caste

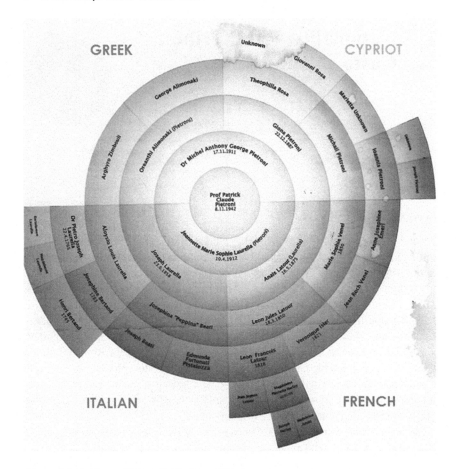

Figure 1.1 Professor Pietroni's Heritage Wheel

the island. Sir Malcolm Stevenson landed in Cyprus and raised the Union Jack and was declared the first British Governor of Cyprus. My mother was the first of our family to obtain British Nationality and we all followed suit.

The island of Cyprus by then had a population of about half a million; 80% Greek and 20% Turkish. Three other small communities also existed: Jewish, Armenian and we, because of the Roman Catholic link, were labelled as Latins – the Latins of Cyprus.

In 1954, the Greek Cypriot community sought their independence from Britain and voted for Enosis (link with Greece). A National terrorist anti-British colonial movement (EOKA) began and we were all issued with identity cards.

Nationality, Race, Tribes, Caste 7

Figure 1.2 Professor Pietroni's Identity Papers

For some reason the designation of "Latin" was not available and my identity card (see image 2) was labelled *Cypriot Other*. Thus I grew up tagged with the label "other" and now seventy years later I have written this book which charts how this label has enabled me to explore and own my "self – my many selves".

Peter Brooks, in his own magisterial book, *The Enigmas of Identity*,[3] follows the journeys undertaken by Proust, Freud and Rousseau in their own exploration of their identity. Brook, in chapter after chapter, charts with examples of their voluminous work and its impact on their lives.

I, dear reader, have chosen to use my own journey in order to illustrate and interrogate what should be considered a form of "work in progress". Each chapter tackles a different aspect of my "otherness" and has influenced my "many identities". We are all both "shaper and the shaped" of our identities and the journey is never finalised.

Evolution and Identity

Born in Cyprus
Small Island in the Mediterranean
Part of the British Empire.

Four Grandparents
All different nationalities
Identity Card says

8   *Nationality, Race, Tribes, Caste*

CYPRIOT-OTHER

Seeking safety
Decided British was best
Sang Rule Britannia
Joined the British Army

Woke up one day
And added R to evolution.

Now smoke a pipe (English)
Drink Ricard (French)
Eat Feta and olives (Greek)
Love Opera (Italian)
Sabbatical in Cincinnati (America)
Lived in Ashram (Namaste)

Still time to discover more
And evolve into what?
A gardener of my
Inherited seeds and
Discovered loves.

Some Great Thinker Wrote
An interpenetrating harmonious mix up.
No need for the
Tyranny of one identity

Learn to live with the wound
Of not knowing who you are.
But continue to discover
Who you can become.

Patrick Pietroni[4]

From the age of ten or so I became a fanatic stamp collector; inheriting both my father's and grandfather's collections. I chose to focus solely on the stamps of the UK and the British Empire (an interest that has never left me). All stamp collectors know the pleasure of possessing all the stamps of one printing i.e. all the stamps printed to commemorate the Golden Jubilee of King George V or the coronation of Queen Elizabeth II. I only recently realised the significance of the word "stamp" in relation to my search for identity. Collecting stamps can, and did, in my case, become a substitute for my own search for identity. Not quite as symbolic as the *Pilgrim's Progress*[5] or Hermann Hesse's *The Journey to the East.*[6] It, however,

Nationality, Race, Tribes, Caste 9

Figure 1.3 Certificate of British Nationality

began my immersion in all things English. I summarise my pre-occupation and immersion in this task with some vignettes, as I stamped myself "a colonial boy".

a. I read all the "*William*" books (Richmal Crompton), *Biggles, Bulldog Drummond, Enid Blyton, WWII heroic stories, Colditz, Reach for the Sky, the Desert Rats, Sherlock Holmes, P.G. Woodhouse.*
b. Aged 16 I joined the local English Youth Club and fell in love with the daughter of an RAF squadron leader. I considered this to be my card of entry to becoming English.
c. I listened to the BBC World Service and followed Arsenal (which I still support). My favourite occupation was to listen to Test Match Special, and I started collecting pictures of the famous bowlers and batsmen, even though I only played cricket sporadically at school. However, I was made captain of the cricket team as everybody thought I was English.
d. At the English school where we were all sent from the age of 13, I won the spoken English prize, reading the poem *The Listeners* by Walter de la Mare.[7]
e. We attended the Queen's Birthday Parade every year and my father signed the Governor's New Year book each January 1st, the sign of loyalty to the British Crown.

10 *Nationality, Race, Tribes, Caste*

f. I forgot to include one of my most precious possessions – an invitation by the Governor of Cyprus to Master Pietroni (aged five) to the Christmas party held at Government House.

I think I have given enough examples to indicate how important my need was to be thought of as English/British, even though none of my ancestors had any link to the United Kingdom.

At the English School there were three or four actual English boys attending. I heard them talk about "going home" in the summer and that begun my drive to go to England, as if it were my home.

Although not very successful in my final exams aged 17 I was accepted as a medical student at Guy's Hospital in London and set foot in England in September 1960. My two older brothers were already at Guy's Hospital, and the family link was all that was required to ensure my acceptance.

I arrived in England expecting to have to buy a bowler hat and read The Times newspaper. I pronounced GROSVENOR Square as it was spelt and not as it was spoken GROVENOR Square. I was soon wearing the clothes that signalled that I was English (blazer, cravat, with top button of shirt open, cuff links and polished George boots as shoes). I began smoking a pipe, which I still do. This was only the beginning of turning myself into an English Gentleman (I had read all of P.G. Wodehouse books on Bertie Wooster and Jeeves by then).

In 1960, at medical school, in my year there were 80–90 boys and 10–12 girls. The competition to "pull", "go out with" and "land" one of the women was great and following a drunken Guy Fawkes party (5 November) in our second year I found myself in the arms (we only "necked" in those days) of the most sought after of the ten women in our year. Not only had she gone to Roedean (the female equivalent of Eton) she was the daughter of a vicar, living in an old traditional vicarage. My English credentials were increasingly rapidly. I had by then given up any pretence at a religious belief or life, so had to cover up my possible unacceptability by suddenly discovering a passion for English church architecture and brass rubbing. We married whilst we were still medical students and before our wedding her father organised a unique service where I converted from being a Roman Catholic to now swearing allegiance to the Church of England (in passing, I must admit that my wife's mother saw through me from the start and never felt I was good enough for her beautiful daughter). So, I upped my charade and applied to join the Royal Army Medical Corps (RAMC) as a medical student, and, given that only the least intelligent medical students tended to apply, I became Captain Pietroni and won all the prizes at the end of my induction training (I continue this story in the chapter on education), and also my final achievement of seeking the status of Britishness, when for ten years or so I became Prince Charles' medical advisor – and he wrote the forward to my book *The Greening of Medicine.*[8]

Nationality, Race, Tribes, Caste 11

Before exploring these other phases of my journey this chapter will end by exploring some of the equally important "signifiers" of identity which are linked to nationality (ethnicity, race, tribes and caste).

Section 2: Nationality

Article 15 of the Universal Declaration of Human Rights states

> Everyone has the right to a Nationality and no one shall be arbitrarily deprived of his nationality nor the right to change his nationality.[9]

Citizenship is closely linked to nationality and confers the right to vote, but nationality may not always grant citizenship.

Some designations e.g. Welsh, Scottish may express a "nationality", even though such a country does not exist by international law. On the other hand, having a British or UK passport has until recently granted the holder to acquire European

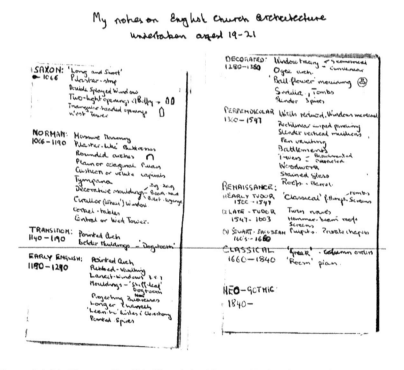

Figure 1.4 My Notes on English Church Architecture Undertaken Aged 19–21

12 Nationality, Race, Tribes, Caste

citizenship. One of the consequences of Brexit has meant that UK citizens no longer possess this "international" designation (European citizenship). Many Cypriots who obtained British nationality are seeking to reclaim their Cypriot nationality (born in Cyprus) in order to possess a European passport as well. There are six forms of British nationality, but not all confer citizenship of the United Kingdom (Hong Kong is the current example of this term "British Nationality", and may well change as a result of the Chinese "take over" of Hong Kong).

Ethnicity

The academic debate regarding both the meaning and definition of ethnicity has never arrived at an agreed description. For some it relates to:

a. A shared descent
b. A shared language
c. Shared activities and customs
d. Shared religion

Two of the major academics in this field, Eriksen and Weber, take a different view and view ethnicity as a construct and ever changing groupings which are influenced by the particular group's interest influenced by social, political and geographical changes. The academic terms used "perpetual perenialism, situation perenialism and instrumental perenialism", may not be particularly helpful to the uninitiated in the academic debates, but essentially my understanding is that some will link the term ethnicity to inherited attributes and some will believe the link to current social political factors will bear on how to classify the different ethnic groups. The debates are further complicated by the confusion and lack of clarity between the term ethnicity and race (see next section). At this point it is helpful to hold onto Martin Bulmer's final statement in his chapter, *Race and Ethnicity*, published in *Key Variables in Social Investigation*. He writes,

> The struggle for a satisfactory classification will continue, made more necessary by the general recognition that Britain is now, as it was not in 1950, a multi-ethnic society whose racial minorities are preponderantly indigenous and British.[10]

Race and Racial

The essential factors that are linked to the terms race and racial are in contrast to ethnicity (social and cultural) are physical and genetic. The physical characteristic most often used to classify race, skin colour, facial features, hair texture and spoken language (accent). Political persuasion is now more commonly used e.g. Black is Beautiful, Black Lives Matter. The period of the European Empire and

Nationality, Race, Tribes, Caste 13

colonialism helped to describe, classify and "invent" the concept of racial groupings. Blumenbach in his book, *On the Natural Varieties of Mankind*[11] identified five different major classifications: Caucasoid, Mongoloid, Negroid, American Indian and Malayan. Since then, many more attempts have been made for political, legal, national, medical and local reasons. There was, and still is, no agreed international classification of the term "race" e.g. in South Africa; until the abolition of apartheid, only three classifications existed: Black, White and Coloured.

The Brazilian government recognises the following classifications: brancos (White), pardos (multi-racial), bretos (Black) and Amardos (Asian). For many years, America used the term "not one drop of blood" in order to claim the racial class of White.

The term "racial essentialism" was introduced by anthropologists in the early part of the 20th Century. The underlying belief of this term was that race was an entirely biological phenomenon. The term "scientific racism" for a while dominated the understanding and management of race; the horrors of the Nazi use of this term in relation to the Jewish "race" in Germany finally ended the emphasis on biology.

From 1970 onwards, the issues regarding human differences were increasingly recognised as cultural and that "racial" gene pools did not exist. Increasingly, and under political as well as social pressure, the word race and racial began to lose favour. Increasingly, the word race became replaced by the terms ethnic and ethnicity.

In a directive in 2000, the Council of the European Union declared,

The European Union rejects theories which attempt to determine the existence of separate human races.[12]

In 2019, the American Association of Physical Anthropologists declared,

Race does not provide an accurate representation of human biological variation. It was never accurate in the past, and it remains inaccurate when referencing contemporary human populations. Humans are not divided biologically into distinct continental types or racial genetic clusters. Instead, the Western concept of race must be understood as a classification system that emerged from, and in support of, European colonialism, oppression, and discrimination.[13]

It became increasingly clear that much of the academic and research writings on the subject of race needed to be rewritten and Bulmer in his chapter on *Race and Ethnicity* uses the following quote from Petersen,

One of the most frequent routes from theory to research is the selection of an indicator appropriately paired with a concept. . . . (T)he unwary researcher easily falls into traps hidden in the deceptively simple definitions of such designations as 'race'. . . . There is no uniquely correct way to define terms

14 *Nationality, Race, Tribes, Caste*

like these. . . . Only painstaking care can help one avoid such traps. . . . (But) there is no reason to deduce from the complexity of an ethnic structure that no classification is feasible

(Petersen 1969b:873, 975).[14]

He ends his chapter with the following,

The struggle for a satisfactory classification will continue, made more necessary by the general recognition that Britain is now, as it was not in 1950, a multi-ethnic society whose racial minorities are preponderantly indigenous and British.[15]

Tribes and Tribalism

These two words are far less controversial than *race* and *racial*. This is mostly because they are identified as a normal and frequent occurrence in the organisation of the members of the human species. Definitions include:

1. Groupings with shared interests, lifestyles and habits.
2. The human tendency and need to form groupings that provide for shared activities, shared geographical location and shared (religious) beliefs.
3. Tribes can and are strongly linked with kinship, family connections and shared language.
4. Some "tribes" will form around political shared beliefs e.g. Democrat/Republican or be supporters of the same sport team – "Arsenal" or the Dodgers.
5. In the film *Crocodile Dundee*, when Mick arrives in New York, he asks his Black chauffer, "*What tribe are you from, mate?*" But in the reply he receives back a look of surprise and confusion.
6. Studies suggest that tribal/social grouping is limited by the primate brain structure and that we are only able to feel "safe" in group sizes of less than 150. This figure is disputed by other studies that indicate that the number is often related to the personality of the "connector" or leader of the tribe. The concept of tribalism is overladen with the tendency for discrimination towards other tribes and is often understood as being the cause of competitive and discriminatory behaviour. Unlike race, tribalism is not associated with physical features of its members. However, identifying factors e.g. flags, items of clothing or the singing of a particular song will help to identify members of a tribe. Inter-tribal conflicts, battles and wars are observed and studied for as long as the human species has existed on planet earth. We are by nature a social animal and by nature we find members of others tribes as potential rivals for food, shelter, territory and sexual gains.

Caste

This last categorisation of the social identifier of the human species has created has been reintroduced by the work of Isabel Wilkerson in her excellent book *Caste: The Origins of our Discontents.*[16] Her work is ground breaking, thorough and will prove to unlock many of the blocks that exist in our current re-examination of "race relations" in the West. Wilkerson unlocks the phrases "unconscious bias" and "the invisible obvious". She describes in great detail the similarities between the caste system in India, the United States and Nazi Germany. I found Wilkerson's arguments detailed and compelling. She writes,

A caste system is an artificial construction, a fixed and embedded ranking of human value that sets the presumed supremacy of one group against the presumed inferiority of other groups on the basis of ancestry and often immutable traits, traits that would be neutral in the abstract but are ascribed life-and-death meaning in a hierarchy favouring the dominant caste whose forebears designed it. A caste system uses rigid, often arbitrary boundaries to keep the ranked groupings apart, distinct from one another and in their assigned places.[16]

She continues,

Throughout human history, three caste systems have stood out. The tragically accelerated, chilling, and officially vanquished caste system of Nazi Germany. The lingering, millennia-long caste system of India. And the shape-shifting, unspoken, race-based caste pyramid in the United States. Each version relied on stigmatizing those deemed inferior to justify the dehumanization necessary to keep the lowest-ranked people at the bottom and to rationalize the protocols of enforcement. A caste system endures because it is often justified as divine will, originating from sacred text or the presumed laws of nature, reinforced throughout the culture and passed down through the generations.[17]

I would add for UK readers that the British class system as typified by the wonderful sketch in the Frost Report (1966) starring David Frost, John Cleese, Ronnie Barker and Ronnie Corbett, although very humorous reminds us that the UK has a caste/class system that is alive and well.

Section 3

Finally, I will try and outline where I believe my identity resides in the five classifications described in this chapter.

Ethnicity

Because most of my ancestors were either born or lived in the Eastern Mediterranean, I might use that designation, as some of my first cousins do. However, the notion of the label Latins appeals to me but is not quite accurate. The geographical name of the region most closely linked to my past generations is

16 *Nationality, Race, Tribes, Caste*

Levantine. The three major cities that were considered to exist and where many of my ancestors lived includes Beirut, Alexandria and Smyrna.

> Diversity and flexibility were the essence of Levantine cities. They could be escapes from the prisons of nationality and religion. In these cities between worlds, people switched identities as easily as they switched languages.[18]

In our family gatherings in Cyprus, it was not unusual for three, four languages to be spoken which all of us could understand.

> The Levant was also a mentality. It put deals before ideals. For the Middle East, Levant and Levantinism were the equivalent of what Patrick Leigh Fermor sees as the role of Romiosyne – the Byzantine world and attitudes which survived under the Ottoman Empire – for Greece: standing for a world of 'shifts and compromises', 'a preference for private ambition over wider aspiration', for empiricism over dogma. Some considered Levantines 'synonymous with duplicity'. Others admired Levantines precisely for their lack of ideals. Thackeray liked Smyrna, which he visited in 1839, because 'there is no fatigue of sublimity about it'.[19]

Another definition of a Levantine was "a rootless individual who takes root wherever he finds himself" – that seems to fit!

Race

Sticking to the biological and physical descriptions I would fit into the term Caucasian, which I tick on forms that still ask that question. The use of this designation is rapidly disappearing and being replaced by the word White, or indeed European.

Tribe

Although there is no such tribe as Cypriot, you are either Greek Cypriot or Turkish Cypriot, I think I would claim to belong to the Latin tribe (community) in Cyprus.

Caste

Having a British nationality living and working in the UK, Europe and the USA, I would use the term class and consider myself as middle class.

Notes

1 A. Maalouf (2008). *Origins*. London. Picador.
2 H. Luke (1965). *Cyprus*. London. George G. Harrap.
3 P. Brooks (2011). *Enigmas of Identity*. Princeton. Princeton University Press.
4 P. Pietroni (2020). *The Poetry and the Evolution of Compassion*. Albuquerque. Fresco Books.
5 J. Bunyan (2003. Originally published 1678). *The Pilgrim's Progress*. New York. Dover Publications.
6 H. Hesse (2003. Originally published 1932). *The Journey to the East*. London. Picador.
7 W. De La Mare (1986. Originally published 1944). The Listeners. In *The Collected Poems of Walter de la Mare*. London. Faber & Faber.
8 P. Pietroni (1990). *The Greening of Medicine*. London. Victor Golancz.
9 Universal Declaration of Human Rights, Article 15 (1948). Available at: www.un.org/en/about-us/universal-declaration-of-human-rights. Last accessed: May 2022.
10 M. Bulmer (1986). Race and Ethnicity. In R. G. Burgess (Ed.). *Key Variables in Social Investigation*. Ch. 4, p. 72. Milton. Routledge and Kegan Paul.
11 J. F. Blumenbach (1969). *On the Natural Varieties of Mankind*. New York. Bergman Publishers.
12 EU Monitor (2000). *Directive 2000/43 – Implementation of the Principle of Equal Treatment Between Persons Irrespective of Racial or Ethnic Origin*. Available at: www.eumonitor.eu/9353000/1/j9vvik7m1c3gyxp/vitgbgi6x6z8. Last accessed: May 2022.
13 American Association of Biological Anthropologists (2019). *AABA Statement on Race & Racism*. Available at: https://physanth.org/about/position-statements/aapa-statement-race-and-racism-2019/. Last accessed: May 2022.
14 Bulmer (1986). *Op. Cit*.
15 Bulmer (1986). *Ibid*.
16 I. Wilkerson (2020). *Caste: The Origins of Our Discontents*. New York. Random House.
17 Wilkerson (2020). *Ibid*.
18 P. Mansel (2010). *Levant: Splendour and Catastrophe on the Mediterranean*. London. John Murray.
19 Mansel (2010). *Ibid*.

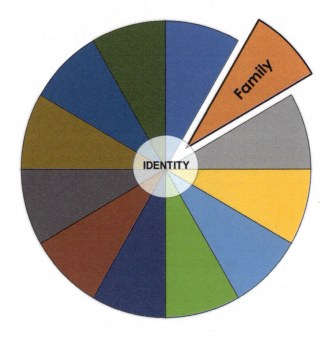

Figure 2.0

2 Family, Social

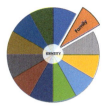

Figure 2.0

Section 1: Biography

My family grew up in Cyprus. My father returned from his medical studies in Paris and married my mother (who was born in Cyprus in 1916). My father worked initially for the Colonial Government and elected to join the British Army during the Second World War (Royal Army Medical Corps – RAMC). At the end of the war, he left the British Army and established himself as a general practitioner in Nicosia (Capital of Cyprus). Our home was in the old walled city, his medical practice was on the ground floor and our home was on the first floor of a newish house with three bedrooms, balconies overlooking the Roman Catholic Church and opposite the Roman Catholic school that was run by the nuns. Our mother, as was the custom, never worked, and we had a series of "servants", both Greek and Turkish, and my father had a secretary and chauffeur as he was the medical officer for the American hospital located in the North of Cyprus, near to the coast.

Our father, to use a polite phrase, was "old fashioned". He used to deliver punishment at three different levels; go stand in the corner (*va au coin*). This entailed us having to face the wall with our hands behind our back, and we could stay like that for hours until he came up from seeing his patients and releasing us. The second level punishment was to be shut in our bedroom (*à ta chambre*) and the third was a caning (*va chercher la canne*). This entailed our going to my parents' bedroom and delivering a "whittle" branch that was used to hit you on your palm or calves.

By this time there were four of us, all boys, and 10 years separated the eldest brother from the youngest. I was the third son (there is a rather large literature on birth order theory which I will explore on the impact on how it may influence personality and identity).

At this point, my own understanding is that I became, and continued to be well into adulthood, my fathers most loved and accepted son. Again my understanding for this had very little to do with me, but occurred because of my mother's depression after my birth. My mother's second son she had hoped

DOI: 10.4324/9781003401414-3

20 *Family, Social*

would be a girl, and indeed she used girl's clothes to dress him in at a very young age. When I was born she withdrew into her bedroom and I was not breastfed, as would have been the custom. Two of my aunts acted as surrogate mothers, and I developed a closer emotional relationship with them until my teenage years. During this time my father "held me" and played with me – before I was old enough to be caned! When this did occur the canings were much milder than those he inflicted on my three brothers, especially Brother no. 2 and Brother no. 4.

An incident on the night of the birth of my brother, Brother no. 4, has had a damaging and long-standing effect in our relationship. On the night of his birth my father took us all, including a cousin staying with us, to see my mother and the new-born. I was only five years old and not allowed to enter the hospital. It was in December; night had begun and I was left in the car on my own in the dark. I cried, wet myself and this was the beginning of my regular night terrors and bed-wetting that lasted seven years. More importantly, I developed an understandable unconscious dislike for my younger brother and I behaved badly towards him, as he puts it, "*I am fed up with all the crap you have unleashed on me over the years*". Birth order theory may explain my behaviour, but my own realisation may have come too late to repair my misdemeanours.

My younger brother was also the most badly assaulted by our father, and on one occasion my father had to be stopped beating him by my mother's brother. My younger brother, understandably, stammered for some years after.

I return to the identity of "brother" at the end of this long biographical introduction.

As well as a brother, I was a son, a father, a husband and now a grandfather. All these identities are framed and influenced by the family and sociocultural factors in which they were manifest. I will continue my own version of these different roles.

Son

When my father had his second heart attack, he was a practicing solo general practitioner in London. I resigned from the RAMC and acted as his locum during his recovery period. My wife and I had two children by then and we moved into a new home close to where my parents lived and my father's general practice. I was thus able to look after my parents for 15–20 years, and was certainly "closest" to them.

My father returned to his practice and we worked together with my wife for some years.

Another "incident" occurred in the practice that caused, and had major repercussions (The son stands up to the father): one morning during seeing patients I could hear my father shouting using the "N-word" at our Jamaican receptionist who had given him the wrong notes. After finishing seeing my patient, I asked my father to apologise to the receptionist. When he refused, I asked him to leave and not return for at least two weeks. This episode caused much family turmoil, and I suspect it may have been categorised as "like father, like son". He eventually came back to work and we grew closer together as I looked after him during his final heart attack. I was also able to look after my mother when she lived for a further ten years before she died. I add some further comments on the father/son relationship in the second section.

Husband

I have been divorced twice and clearly have not been party to successful marriages. I would add (possibly), to diminish the guilt and embarrassment, that I have remained (mostly) on very good terms with my ex-wives.

Father

My wife and I had three children and the marriage ended when they were eight, six and three. I left our home, and a year later, the family practice that we worked in together. By that time my younger brother had joined us. Divorces are never "good" and this one was not awful, but not at all easy. Before the divorce we shared the parenting together, we had a live-in mother's help, and my most pleasant memory was celebrating my wife's 30th birthday with a big family party, just before our marriage ran into trouble. I loved being a father of a young family, but believe I was more at ease with my sons than with my daughter. Our youngest son developed polio (from the vaccine) at three months and required several hospital admissions and much surgery to enable him to walk without a calliper. We sang together, we cooked together and we played together. More challenges and difficulties arose after the divorce, when I remarried two years after the separation. The children had to get used to two homes and a new "mother figure", as well as a new "father figure" as my ex-wife also found a new partner, although they never married. I decided to leave the family practice to my ex-wife and younger brother and worked for a general practice night service so I could pick-up and take my children to school two to three times a week. My second wife was immensely helpful and involved with the care of three young children, which had its difficulties, certainly for them, as well as their mother. It would be fair to say the arrangement continued to be "bumpy". Guilt was never far away, and still remains to this day, and most harm was done to our daughter having to grow up with two very different and challenging mother and step-mother. A low ebb in my role as husband and father, and without doubt one of the major factors for the second divorce, my children were by then married and grandchildren born (the second marriage lasted 36 years). A twice divorced "husband" is an identity I feel most ashamed of and it remains so.

22 *Family, Social*

Grandfather

Of all the roles so far this became, and has been, the most enjoyable. Family holidays in France, with swimming pool, tennis court, horse riding. Every summer when the seven grandchildren, plus two to four friends' children came and created "The Lion Gang" and wrote and performed a play for the parents at the end of the holiday. I remember *Dumbledory*, a skit on Harry Potter. Now half are at university and half finishing school. I keep in contact with them all through a monthly *Letters from America/Shrewsbury* or wherever I am. I have refused to take part in Zoom or other digital offerings and several of the grandchildren will reply to my "letter" and will visit us in the summer with boyfriend or girlfriend in tow.

Grandson

I can remember my father's parents well and have only a fleeting memory of my mother's mother. The most distinct memory of her was that I was not allowed to go to her funeral. Aged between 10 and 14 I spent several summer holidays with my father's parents with whom I spoke in Greek or French. My grandmother went to the Greek Orthodox Church, whereas my grandfather went to the Roman Catholic Church on Sundays. My grandparents lived in the town of Kyrenia on the north coast of Cyprus and he was the managing director of a factory that made olive oil. He would take me every day to the factory which was on the coast and made me addicted to singing in the car (which I continued along with my own children and grandchildren to their acute embarrassment). The factory was on the sea shore and he taught me to swim and dive. He wore those old-fashioned swimming costumes that you see in old films of people bathing in the Victorian era. When we returned from the factory in the early evening, my grandmother would have arranged his cold drink of ouzo (Pernod) and a plate of peeled cucumber with salt. The cucumber peel was on a separate plate, and as I am writing this I can picture him snapping the cucumber and the sound of his crunching it with his teeth – a habit I have copied myself to this day. I remember him taking me into his office and pointing to the sculpture of the three monkeys – *hear no evil, see no evil, speak no evil*, a sculpture I have had on my desk as well.

Cousin and Nephew

My father was the eldest of five and we had 11 cousins. We would meet over Christmas and Easter, usually at my aunt's (my father's sister), who had married a very successful Armenian businessman who had escaped the massacre of Armenians in 1908 in Turkey. He was a very impressive individual, and we young cousins called him Chik-Chak. He owned the first green Chrysler car that appeared in Cyprus, and also had a maze in his large and wonderful house where we would all meet. At Christmas he would come into the room where all the cousins were and give us each one pound (a HUGE amount in those days).

My father's younger brother was married to a beautiful Polish lady with whom I had a secret wish that she was my mother. His children were my closest cousins. As a family, they would drive to the coast every Sunday to swim and I joined them. In many ways I often wished I belonged to their family, rather than mine. I never remember my father in casual open-necked shirt, until I was about 16, when, for the first time we went to Greece on a cruise (my eldest brother was in London, studying medicine).

Friends and Friendship

I truly believe that the competitive atmosphere created by my father influenced me to the extent that close male friendships came late in my life, and it was friendship with women that allowed me to share my emotional life, something I have only found possible in the sixth and seventh decade.

At school, my closest friend between ages six to 17 was Haro Bedelian, the son of a cultured man (who did the Times crossword). Haro and I competed for 1st and 2nd place in our class exam. He went on to build the Channel Tunnel for which he has been rightly awarded the CBE (I am sure you can read between the lines that I am still competing with him!).

I consider myself very fortunate that the friendship that existed with my two divorced wives has allowed us to continue a friendship which is occasionally under attack, but has been sustained all these years. All my close male friends of my 60's and 70's have died, and I no longer have the pleasure of playing chess or bridge and discussing the state of our politics or listening to Mahler's 5th symphony with them.

Section 2: Literature Overview

Families and Groups

One of the major 'balancing acts' we have to perform in our lives is the one between our own individual needs and the needs of the family, group, society or nation we live in. No man is an island, yet living on an island and getting away from it all is a frequent fantasy for all of us. The family unit serves in some way as the transition between the individual's needs and the needs of the group. In all the 4000 societies present on earth, the family unit forms the base to that society. Experiments with other 'units' such as the kibbutz in Israel or the communes in the United States have generally not developed past their experimental stage. Most of us will have been born into a family (family of origin) and the majority of us will go on to find a mate and create our own family unit. There has been a dramatic decrease in the extended family (more than two generations living together) and

24   *Family, Social*

even the nuclear family (two parents plus children) has a less frequent pattern than two decades ago. With the increase in divorce, many more single-parent families exist and there has also been an increase in experimental family units with gay men and lesbian women living together and raising their own children.

Each culture has its own pattern of family "style", but it is possible to detect certain recurring patterns which may help you to identify your own family.

Closed Family

In this sort of family, the "rules" are well-known and relatively rigid. "You brush your teeth every morning before breakfast" or "No one is to stay out later than 10 pm". Each family has its own sets of rules, but in a closed family these do not evolve and usually one or other parent is relatively authoritarian. The family appears close-knit and does not accept strangers easily. Attempts by individuals in the family to break out and rebel are usually punished and the family may well collectively side against the rebel and expel him from the family. The rebel may feel rejected, unwanted, and if his attempts to join another unit at school or group at work are similarly unsuccessful, he may develop the "outsider" mentality that has been so well captured by books like *Religion and the Rebel*[1] and *The Outsider* (Colin Wilson).[2]

Random Family

Here the reverse is true: the family does not have a feeling of being a family, either because of constant conflict between husband and wife or because of a false understanding of the need for permissiveness. Everyone is allowed to do "their own thing". The family operates more like a collection of individuals than a unit pulling together. Birthdays and holidays are not jointly celebrated and the rituals and ceremonies present in a closed family are absent. Paradoxically, watching television can help to fragment a closed family but can also bring a random family closer together. Often, watching television together is the nearest a random family gets to having a group ritual.

Open Family

This is a mixture of these two extremes: the need for individual growth and separateness is recognised whilst at the same time the boundaries of the family group are protected and preserved. Parents learn from their children and alter the family rituals to take into account new interests and new friends, whilst children respect the need to maintain the stability of the family and enjoy continuing the traditions when they form their own families.

The balance between the needs of the individual and the needs of the group (family-community) is mirrored in political attitudes, with one political party stressing the importance of the individual freedom and responsibility whilst the other places a great emphasis on central government control and community care. The manner in which we each "survive" our family of origin and create our own may well influence the pattern of our approach to the political solutions we support.

Family Cycle

Like an individual, each family goes through various stages of development, each with its own pleasures and problems. Understanding the ebb and flow of family life may well help prevent the frustration and pain when your own family is under stress or in a crisis. The family of origin is the family you were born into. The first step in creating your own family involves some separation and disengagement either when you leave school or get married. This disengagement process can be made problematic depending on the closeness or randomness of your family of origin. Establishing your own relationship with a fellow human being is the first step in creating your own family unit. How many of your own "rules" do you bring with you? How does your mate adapt to your style?

For new couples, this phase of the family life cycle is where the majority of these issues will first be encountered. This stage may be made more difficult by financial or housing difficulties and if the young couple are still living with either set of parents, being on their own can be made that much more problematic. The next stage involves the arrival of children and for many couples today, with adequate contraception, this stage does not need to coincide with the previous stage. Nevertheless, the arrival of children shifts the focus of the family life from the needs of the adults to those of the young arrivals. Patterns of work, sleep, sex and feeding are usually altered and the young couple begin to develop their own rules and rituals and lay down the foundations for a more or less closed/open-random family.

The next stage involves the children going to school or the wife returning to work or both. Children begin to develop their own personalities, likes and dislikes and the "family" begins to shape its own characteristics, with decisions on where to go on holiday, how to spend Christmas, who does the washing up etc. One in four marriages will by now have ended in divorce, and the conflicts, pain and distress that result from the break will force both parents and children to face the dissolution of the family unit. How this is handled will be more important than that it has happened. Can the parents avoid blaming each other, especially in front of the children? Can the parents agree to a mutually acceptable "division"? Will each parent agree to the other visiting and having access? How will they explain the divorce to the children? If there is another person, how much will he or she be involved in caring for the children? The answers to these and many other questions will influence both the children of the first

26 *Family, Social*

marriage and any children of subsequent marriages. Two in five children now have step-parent, and the complexities of creating a stable family unit in second marriages are even more difficult than in a first marriage.

Having survived this stage and gone back to start again, couples are faced with the children leaving home and the "empty nest" syndrome. The role the mother has had during the early phases will greatly influence what kind of challenges may have to be face. This is the time when the man leaves with his secretary or younger woman, leaving a 40–50 year old who has given her life to the family alone, desperate without a job and little identity. It can also be the time when the couple rediscover the joys of being on their own without the demands of children, their home paid for and cared for. They find that being in the company of another human being who has shared a lifetime of pleasure and pain, sorrow and joy, is indeed one of the greatest achievements known to the human species. They approach the next stages of their life together – retirement and the threat of bereavement – with an equanimity found only in those who are at peace, not only with themselves, but with their follow human beings.

Birth Order Theory

This was first proposed by Alfred Adler (1870–1937)[3] who was one of the original colleagues of Freud and Jung. Adler focussed his writings on power and hierarchy and his birth-order theory suggested that the first-born were powerful figures, acting as the successor to the father, as in Royal families. The middle children were often overlooked and ignored, and the younger children pampered, spoilt or neglected. This theory is no longer considered to be correct. Subsequent research studies have been unable to identify an alternative theory and the studies suggest that birth order has little influence on the development of identity and personality. Many large studies have consistently failed to identify a consistent pattern that supports any birth order theory. Notwithstanding the paucity of any good evidence to support a "general birth-order theory", too many individual stories, too many novels and plays suggest that there remains a strong belief in its existence. I for one believe that my being the third son of a four son family had a substantial effect on my personality. No mention has so far been made regarding the difference as to what sibling sexual difference may have on a birth-order theory (see section 3).

Family Dynamics, Family Relationships and Illness

Much of this section will draw on my own medical experience as a family doctor in London over many decades. I will also draw on my extensive study of the different healthcare systems in Europe, United States and Cuba. Robert Rakel and David Rakel in their comprehensive book, *Textbook of Family Medicine*[4]

Family, Social   27

provide an excellent overview of this area of clinical work. I start with three vignettes from my own practice:

1. The widower with arthritic knees

    An elderly Bangladeshi man came to see me with painful knees. The examinations indicated he had mild arthritis and I prescribed some cream to rub on the knees. He returned the following week and asked for an x-ray which showed he had mild arthritis. The following week when he returned asking for a specialist referral I asked him, "Do you have difficulty when you pray?" His face lit up and he said, "My wife died last month and I go to the mosque to pray and be with her, but it becomes too painful." I suggested I would phone the senior Muslim Director of the mosque and suggest he be allowed to sit and pray in the mosque. This was agreed and he returned (with presents) to thank me.

2. Who is the patient and what is the problem?

    A young mother brought her four year old boy to see me with what appeared to be a minor cold. He looked unhappy, as did the mother who requested antibiotics. I examined the child and noted his chest and lungs were clear. I asked the mother why she decided to bring him to the doctor. She said, "My husband is on night work and came home and heard Jimmy cry and cough. He shouted at me, 'Take him to the doctor today, how can I sleep with him coughing? You must look after him better than you have.'" She then burst into tears.

    Clearly the problem was not with the child, who was by now clutching his mother, but with the marriage.

3. <u>Learning from experience</u>

    Following morning surgery, the GPs (six) would meet to discuss and share out home visits. We had a young trainee doctor with us and I asked him to visit "Mrs Smith", whose husband had just died. He looked at me askance and said, "What can I do? He is dead." I suggested he went. He reported back that Mrs Smith had welcomed him, offered him a cup of tea and spent five minutes thanking him for coming and thanking the "good doctors and nurses" at the practice who had looked after her husband. After five-ten minutes when the doctor had said nothing, she said, "You are very kind to have come, but I have kept you too long talking and you must be very busy." The doctor left without saying anything, not examining her, and not prescribing.

    Twenty years later, I received a letter from the not-so-young doctor, who wrote and said, "Patrick, that visit you sent me on taught me what being a doctor in the community is all about."

Of the many things I learnt from my father was to always receive all the medical files of the whole family when seeing an individual member. Illness in one member of the family will impact on all members of the family and an understanding of the family dynamics is an important and necessary factor when making a diagnosis or establishing a treatment plan.

28   *Family, Social*

Durall's study identified the following characteristics in families that were more able to cope with illness in one member, be it a child, a parent or grandparent.

1. They approach problems in a unified manner as a family;
2. they have a nonmaterialist orientation;
3. the husband and wife frequently share tasks;
4. they perceive the nature of the problem accurately; and
5. they have a democratic orientation, with diffusion of leadership regarding problem-solving tasks.[5]

Finally, I address some of the more frequent challenges a family doctor will encounter over his professional career (marital conflict, scapegoating and the doll's house family). I have chosen these three as I believe their existence in my family helped to shape and influence aspects of my own identity.

Marital Conflict and Divorce

Divorce was a very uncommon occurrence in the social culture that I grew up in. It was also illegal in the Roman Catholic community in Cyprus. The divorce rate per 1000 population continues to increase as the laws have changed and the position and power balance women have in society is now very different. In the western countries, the rate of divorce is around 20–25% and two thirds of divorces are instigated by the wives.[6]

Divorce laws have not remained static and at-fault divorce is no longer a requirement. No-fault divorce, uncontested divorce and increasing mediated divorce are far more common. The different religions (Christian, Muslim, Hindu) all still have prohibitions regarding divorce and financial settlements. The main causes have not altered over the last 50 years and include:

Extra marital sex   28% (men 75%, women 25%)
Domestic violence   17%
Mid-life crisis   13%[7]

The effect on the children in the marriage has been extensively studied and not only can they become prone to physical symptoms (headaches, stomach aches, crying fits, sleep disturbance), they may exhibit school phobias, outbursts of anger and educational under achievement.

According to Nicholas Wall, former President of the Family division of the English High Court,

> People think that post-separation parenting is easy – in fact, it is exceedingly difficult, and as a rule of thumb my experience is that the more intelligent the parent, the more intractable the dispute. There is nothing worse, for most children than for their parents to denigrate each other. Parents simply do not realise

the damage they do to their children by the battles they wage over them. Separating parents rarely behave reasonably, although they always believe that they are doing so, and that the other party is behaving unreasonably.[8]

Scapegoating

It is not at all unusual in families, especially those with several children, for one of them assigning to be blamed for the dysfunction in the family. Scapegoating allows a family to address the dysfunction by avoiding any problematic discussion by identifying one of the children as always at fault, and the principal causes of the dysfunction. Often this allows the parents to avoid blaming each other, even though they may differ as to which child should be blamed.

Dolls House Family

This often occurs where the wife (as in my family) is a "trophy" wife, and has little or no say in how the family is run. The husband will not only determine the rules of how the children should be treated but also will administer punishment if any child disobeys those rules.

Section 3: Biography-Linking Theory

Families and Groups

I think it would be fair to say that we were a family ruled by a somewhat tyrannical father who felt he was "doing the right thing". The level of punishment and beatings that we all received might have been considered normal, but was too excessive and its effect on all four sons led us all to "copy" father and become doctors. It certainly effected the relationship we developed with him, and my own close identification with him enabled me to join him in his practice. Our mother was a silent member of the family when it came to creating our family style, but we all showed the appropriate affection, if not the respect we might have done, if her role in the family had been different. We all got married soon after qualifying as a doctor. I was the exception and married my fellow medical student in our third year of studies. Our father did not approve of the wives chosen by my two elder brothers, and this caused an increasing split between them and him. Once our father died it became possible for a while for the "family" (four sons and a mother) to experience some form of cohesiveness at birthdays and high days.

Brother and Birth Order Theory

It is clear that the favouritism that our father showed me and my responsiveness to him resulted in my eventual scapegoating. I have had to accept that my response to my younger brother fully justified his own response to my behaviour

30 *Family, Social*

in our family. Birth order theory has much to explain how we were shaped by the "grand shaper", our father.

Birth order theory may also explain why brother 2 and brother 3 developed the closest emotional relationship, which lasts to this day. We were born 18 months apart, whereas the eldest brother was five years older than me and the youngest five years younger.

Son

As a third son, I had many disadvantages and advantages. The fact that our father played a much greater part in my early childhood created a bond that may have been absent for my three brothers. I believe, however, this "special relationship" with him allowed me to stand up to him when he behaved so appallingly to our Jamaican receptionist. This also allowed me to look after him as he was dying and when he passed away with his third heart attack. In some ways I was both the son who stayed at home and also the prodigal son who returned from his travels.

Husband

What sort of a husband have I been and how would each of my ex-wives, and current wife, describe me? How would their descriptions of me differ from mine? I think all I feel comfortable saying about my identity as a husband is that I have felt, and still feel, distressed (guilt and shame) by acknowledging the label "divorced twice" as a description of myself. On both occasions I sought support and comfort from my brothers, their wives and my therapists. Both my father and mother were still alive in the first divorce and proved to be supportive, concerned and accepting.

Father

I have, to a large extent, avoided the mistakes my own father made and enjoy an easy and pleasant contact with all three of my children now aged 55, 53 and 50. I have been more relaxed with my sons than with my daughter, but have turned to her for advice more easily now than before. I realise that not having had a sister, my experience in close friendships with women has only been made possible after my fifth decade. In many ways, I believe I related more to my mother as an older sister rather than a mother.

Grandson

I was happiest when staying with my grandfather.

Grandfather

This has been by far my most enjoyable and comfortable position I have held in the family, and I owe much to my own grandfather's influence on me. He showed me the way to both play and be learned.

Cousin and Nephew

Although never forming close friendships with my cousins, the opportunity I had to experience family outings not led by my own parents provided me with guidance as to how "happy families" can exist. I was especially close to two of my aunts who had looked after me when my mother was disabled by her depression following my birth and the disappointment to her I was not a girl.

Friends and Friendship

My male friends and friendships have all been sprinkled with a competitive approach that has limited their development. This no doubt being a continuation of the competitiveness that existed between myself and my brothers.

It has only been lately in my late sixties and seventies that I believe I learned how to appreciate and love a close male friend. Unfortunately, all of them have passed away. I have been very supported by the wish of their wives and partners who asked me to give the eulogy at their funerals. (A bit late Patrick! But not too late to have appreciated the importance of a small circle of intimate and loving friends.)

Notes

1 C. Wilson (1957). *Religion and the Rebel*. London. Victor Gollancz.
2 C. Wilson (1956). *The Outsider*. London. Victor Gollancz.
3 A. Alder (2011. Originally published 1927). *The Practice and Theory of Individual Psychology*. Eastford. Martino Fine Books.
4 R. E. Rakel & D. P. Rakel (Eds.) (2011). *Textbook of Family Medicine*. Berkeley. Elsevier Saunders.
5 Rakel & Rakel (2011). *Ibid*.
6 Rakel & Rakel (2011). *Ibid*.
7 Rakel & Rakel (2011). *Ibid*.
8 The Times (2020). *How to Separate without Hurting the Children*. 21 September. Available at: www.theguardian.com/lifeandstyle/2010/sep/21/separate-divorce-hurting-children. Last accessed: May 2022.

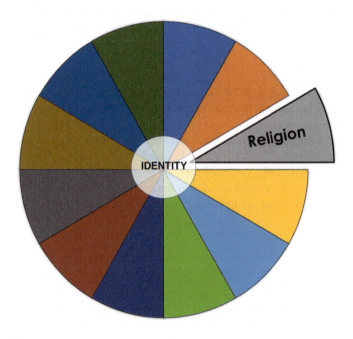

Figure 3.0

3 Religion, Beliefs

Figure 3.0

Section 1: Biography

The five major religions that existed in Cyprus included the Greek Orthodox Church, the Turkish Muslim mosques, the Roman Catholic Church and the smaller Maronite and Armenian Churches. There were also a small number of Jewish synagogues. Our house was sandwiched between the Roman Catholic Church and the Roman Catholic nunnery that doubled as a school (where I attended for a short while). It was clearly not possible for us, as we were growing up, to avoid going to church regularly on Sunday, having confessed our sins on Saturday and not eaten meat on Friday, we were able to take holy communion on Sunday after we had had our first communion ceremony aged 11. I remember that occasion very well, for it was one of the important "rites of passage" in the Roman Catholic Church. The event occurred early in the morning, after we had fasted all night and was followed by a "breakfast" with boiled eggs (my egg was hard boiled).

The Roman Catholic Church first arrived in Cyprus in the 12th Century. Cyprus served as a stopping off base for the third crusade in 1192. King Richard I rescued his bride to be, Berengaria, from the then King of Cyprus and built amazing castles and abbeys that have attracted tourists ever since.

In 2020, an exhibition and booklet was produced by the Government of Cyprus entitled, "*The Latins of Cyprus*", and the following is a shortened history of this community for the past 1000 years that our family formed part of.

> The Latins of Cyprus are Roman-Catholics of Europe or Franco-Levantine descent. This name has prevailed since the Byzantine era, when anyone originating from Western Europe was called a "Latin" because they were related to the area of the ancient Latium in Italy. At the same time, the Greek-speaking Byzantines called themselves Romans (the Byzantium evolved from the Roman Empire), and not Greeks (the ones who embrace polytheism).
>
> The presence of Latins in Cyprus starts with the establishment of the Roman-Catholic Church in the 12th century. Leontios Machairas uses the

DOI: 10.4324/9781003401414-4

34 *Religion, Beliefs*

name "Latins" in his chronicle, to refer to the first crusaders and settlers of Palestine and Cyprus, but also, in general, to refer to the religion of Westerns who are not Greek Orthodox. The first references appeared in 1126, when a huge immigration movement of knights, soldiers and merchants appeared following the conquest of Cyprus by Richard I the Lionheart, and of the sale of Cyprus to Guy de Lusignan. The foundation of the Latin Archbishopric in Nicosia in 1196, along with three Bishoprics in Famagusta, Limassol and Paphos, enhanced the descent of more Roman-Catholic religious orders in Cyprus and, due to the need for the establishment of an empire, these orders were granted assets and multiple benefits. During the Frankish Rule (1191–1489) and the Venetian Rule (1489–1571), the members of those groups were the ruling class of the island and they were mainly roman-Catholics from France, Italy and Palestine.

The persecution of the Roman-Catholic Church by the Ottomans, after the conquest of Cyprus (1570–1571), lead to an almost complete dissolution of the Latin Church, because the Catholics were forced to either embrace Islam, or become members of the Greek-Orthodox dogma, forcing the majority, mainly wealthy bourgeois and clergymen, to abandon Cyprus. Only a small number of Latins remained, who were forced to appear as Orthodox. Soon, however, the relations between the Latin Church and the Ottomans started to recover, since the Most Serene Republic of Venice entered a peace treaty with the Ottoman Rulers in 1573. At the beginning, Frankish monks founded the monasteries of the Holy Cross in Nicosia and the Virgin Mary of Graces in Larnaca (1596). After that, the Ottomans allowed the re-establishment of the Latin Bishopric in Paphos (1629) and the founding of the Terra Santa School in Nicosia (1646). They did not react to the settlement of even more European Roman Catholics on the island, as a consequence of the increasing number of European consulates mainly in Larnaca, which were necessary to strengthen the financial and diplomatic relations between Europe and the East.

During the 18th and 19th centuries, the classes of the European Roman-Catholics of Cyprus, included doctors, bankers and landowners from different nations of the West, in addition to merchants and diplomats. Also, the number of Latin churches and schools increased in all the cities. By the end of the British Rule in Cyprus and the declaration of Independence of the Republic of Cyprus, the Cypriot Roman-Catholics were able to be represented in all the sectors of the Cypriot society.

When the Republic of Cyprus was established, the number of the Latins of Cyprus, according to the census of that year (1960), was 4,505.[1]

I played a small part in collecting the figure of 4,505. In 1960, after Cyprus became an independent country, my uncle (see the following) had by then become

Religion, Beliefs 35

the titular secular leader of the small Roman Catholic community. The constitution for the new government of Cyprus allowed for an elected parliamentary representative for any community with over 5,000 members. My Uncle rounded up all the cousins and sent us to collect signatures from all over the island. Although we fell short of 5,000 souls, strings were pulled in the right quarter and my Uncle Tony was declared the elected representative of the Latin religion group in the House of Representatives and later became the Papal Nuncio for Cyprus.

Representatives of the Latin religious group in the House of Representatives

Anthony Pietroni (1965–1976)

Anthony Pietroni was born in Cairo, Egypt, to a Cypriot father and mother from the Greek island of Chios, on February 2nd, 1913. He graduated from the Law School of the University of Paris, in 1931. He served at the Cyprus Volunteer Force during World War II, from 1941 until 1943. He received the honorary distinctions of Knight of the Cross (1962) and Knight Commander (1966) of the Equestrian Order of the Holy Sepulchre of Jerusalem, as well as Knight Commander of the Order of Saint Gregory the Great (1990). He was married to Halina Nakoniecznikow-Klukowska and they had three children. He passed away on March 13th 1998.

During the elections of July 7th, 1960, he was declared first representative of the Latin religious group in the Greek Communal Chamber, with no other candidate. After the dissolution of the Chamber and the transfer of its legislative power to the House of Representatives, he continued to represent the Latin religious group in the Parliament, with an extended term, until 1970. At the elections that took place on July 19th, 1970, in accordance with the Religious Groups (Representation) Law, he was declared first representative of the Latin group in the House of Parliament, with no other candidate.[2]

My Religious Journey

After my confirmation and first communion, I attended the church (next door) regularly for Catechism lessons on Saturday and holy mass on Sunday.

By the age of 12/13, Brother no. 2 had introduced me to the delights of masturbation, which in my case was to plague me with guilt for many years. This was mostly due to the nature of the priest who sat in the privacy of the confessional box and would start the procedure with, "How many times have you abused yourself my son?" I would respond with a number which was followed with more detailed questions. I soon learnt that my "penance" was a mixture of three to four Hail Mary's and one or two Our Fathers', to be said in Latin. This

36 *Religion, Beliefs*

is the brilliance of the Roman Catholic faith – you sin, you confess, you perform a penance – and then you can start sinning again. It did not take me long to work out that from the shuffling and heavy breathing coming from the priest's closed off box suggested he was himself guilty of a greater sin. I decided to take my sinning to God himself. When I was 15 I told him I would stop masturbating if he would help me get as good results in my end of year exam as my brothers. It worked, I did. However, after two weeks of abstinence, I had a nocturnal emission and cried out to God, "I didn't do it! I promise, didn't do it!" This episode was the end of my religious beliefs and for many years after I read widely and was much helped by William James' book, *"The Varieties of Religious Experience"*.[3] As I describe in the section on Family, I married the daughter of an English vicar and focused on getting to know the beauty of the English country churches and took up brass rubbing as a hobby, and converting to the Church of England and leaving the Roman Catholic Church. My father-in-law was a very wise, well read and kindly man, who introduced me to Teilhard de Chardin and the poet/priest Gerald Manley Hopkins, and the Windhover poem set me free (we named one of our homes in Shropshire, Windhover). Other teachers included Thomas Merton to India, the Bhargava Gita and my pursuit of Eastern philosophy was established.

In 1974, aged 32, I was successful in obtaining a six-month sabbatical at Chapel Hill University in North Carolina. Jimmy Carter was President at the time and keen on supporting the development of family medicine (General Practice). Many young GPs like myself were headhunted to help establish training programmes for American doctors. I was appointed Residency Director and it was intended that the whole family (my wife and our three children) would all go. A month before we were due to leave, my father died and my wife had to stay back as there would have been no one to oversee our now expanding General Practice in Shepherd's Bush, London.

It meant that now after nearly 12 years of marriage we would spend time apart, and it also meant that being alone in Chapel Hill allowed me to pursue my search for "religious experience" with a freedom that I would not have otherwise have had (both good and bad things were to follow). Aged 32, living on my own in the States, I believe I had my delayed adolescence. Fritz Perls, the Encounter Group movement based in California, together with smoking my first joint, unloosed many internal chains, and in a poem I wrote later I added "r" to evolution. More important chains were cut when I received a letter from my wife telling me she wanted a divorce as she had met someone else. This propelled me into even more fragmentation and I returned to the UK with a beard, a ponytail and a thirst for "finding myself". Within two years I left the family practice, met my future wife, a psychotherapist at the Tavistock Clinic, and was offered a more senior role as Director of Family Medicine at the University of Cincinnati. It was during this second period in America that I met Swami Rama, an Indian guru who became my teacher and guide for the next ten years. Swamaji, as he was known to us, had established the Himalayan Institute in what had been a large training school for nuns in Scranton (Pennsylvania). The Institute focused on exploring the training of the Himalayan yogis using Western medical investigating instrumentation. The majority of the student cohort who came to study there were doctors, nurses, psychologists, psychiatrists. Our teaching was supervised by Swamaji and some of his closest disciples, which I also eventually became. Hours of meditation, detailed practicing of pranayama (breathing control), cooking lessons involving Ayurvedic teaching about food, isolation for three to five days on one's own were accompanied by an extensive examination using Western investigative methods (x-ray, electrocardiogram, electroencephalograms, oxygen and carbon dioxide measurements) provided me with an education that I had never had in my own medical training.

The Gita, as we called it, Bhargava Gita became our bible and many of us (not me) learnt to chant and sing the "holy" songs. (The Gita is a collection of Hindi scriptures over 800 years old and is part of a much larger series of books known as Mahabharata).[4]

I also became a teacher at the Himalayan Institute, but to my horror and dismay I learnt that Swamaji was deflowering many of the young women who formed part of his intimate circle under the cover of teaching them Tantric Yoga. A young woman was badly injured by his "teachings"; he was pursued by the girl's parents and he hurried back to India where he died two years later.

As with my father, when I learnt about this episode, I flew back to the Institute when he was still there and confronted him with his behaviour.

My next journey involved my applying to train as a psychoanalyst. I had by then read Freud and Jung in some depth and chose a Jungian analysis as I perceived (rightly) that Jung had himself explored the Hindu texts and written widely on this subject. I continue this story in Chapter 6 where I explore the psychological journey I now embarked on very much influenced by my new wife.

Section 2: Literature Overview

I cannot pretend that in this next section I will cover a history of religious practice, let alone a history of God. If you wish to do so, can I suggest you read some of the many books written by Karen Armstrong, who herself became a good friend and important guide in my own search. A much shorter guide is the book entitled *Religion* by Leszek Kolakowski.[5] He was expelled from Poland in 1968 and the list of universities he then taught at is quite amazing – Yale, McGill, Montreal, Berkley, Oxford and many others. A more recent book by Robert Sapolsky called "*Behave: the biology of humans at our best and worst*"[6] says it all. Nevertheless, here is my take on morality and religion which appears as Section 3.

38 Religion, Beliefs

SKY HOOKS AND OTHER FOLK

Some have always looked to the heavens
to attach their sky hooks.
Gods and Goddesses first, then God – a man, of course.
Then Messengers from God -
Abraham, Jesus, Mohammed.
Some (from the East) have hooked onto
Buddha, Confucius, Atman.
A very few hooked onto Goddesses –
Isis, Artemis, Hera, Aphrodite, Parvati,
Virgin Mary, St. Bernadette.
Then the Philosophers began to Philosophise –
Plato, Socrates, Aristotle.
Zeno of Citium, Avicenna, Maimonides.
The Enlightenment produced more than a few –
Bacon, Descartes, Newton, Galileo, Montaigne.
The end justify the means – I think therefore I am.
And the age of Reason was born –
Leibniz and Spinoza competed over the truth.
The French took over and revolted –
Voltaire, Diderot, Rousseau ruled the roost.

The Brits would have none of it.
They called it Empiricism.
Foretelling the Empire, no doubt.
Locke, Hume and his fork led to
Smith and the market.
Kant founded the metaphysics of morals.
Burke introduced utilitarianism
and debated with Paine, but added
The greatest good for the greatest number.
Hegel and Marx disagreed over mind and spirit.
Schopenhauer introduced us to the East
(Remember the Dalai Llama is still alive).

I would like to finish soon, but must mention
The three Johns,
John Stuart Mill, John Maynard Keynes, John Rawls
For they still oversee our economy and the market.

Others turned inwards
Searching for their soul

Read Jung, Milton, Wittgenstein,
Hesse, Castaneda and Rumi

You will no doubt notice – very few women
In this list (this may be the problem and may
Also point to the solution).
I will finish with my own favourites –
Mary Wollstonecraft, Simone de Beauvoir,
Hanna Arendt, Luce Irigaray, Julia Kristeva
And of course, Greta Thunberg.

Who will you hitch up with?
A Skyhook for the Gods?
A library full of books?
Remember you can of course always
Change your mind.

Professor Pietroni[7]

Section 3: Biography-Linking Theory

I separate the belief in a religion (the majors being Christianity, Islam, Judaism, Buddhist and Hindu) from a search for the spirit through spiritual practice. The former entails believing in, and following, the "rules" (the shoulds and shouldn'ts) as written in the "good books" – the Bible, Koran, Tora, and Bhargava Gita etc.

The major five religions and their adherents appear to have spent much of their time arguing, fighting, killing, torturing (I could go on) over the centuries since their existence. Even more peculiar, they have turned on members of their own religion; Catholics killed Protestants, Shia killed Sunni etc. So, although I have read many of the good books available and understand the basic tenants and beliefs of the big five, I no longer believe any of the big five had the answers to the questions we seek. However, they do appear to agree on one rule – *The Golden Rule.*

The Golden Rule

That one should treat others as one wishes to be treated oneself, seems both self-evident and is universally accepted as the ethic of responsibility. In *A Dictionary of Philosophy,*[8] its meaning is expanded to include:

a. Do not treat others in ways you would not like to be treated.
b. What you wish upon others, you wish upon yourself.

40 *Religion, Beliefs*

It appears in different forms in all the world's major religion, and its earliest attribution is in an ancient Egyptian text (circa 2040–1650 BCE):

Now this is the command – "Do to the doer to make him do".[9]

The World Religions

Christianity	All things whatsoever ye would that men should do to you, do ye so to them; for this is the law and the prophets – Matthew 7:1
Confucianism	Do not do to others what you would not like yourself. Then there will be no resentment against you, either in the family or in the state. – Analects 12:2
Buddhism	Hurt not others in ways that you yourself would find hurtful – Udana-Varga 5,1
Hinduism	This is the sum of duty; do naught onto others what you would not have them do unto you. – Mahabharata 5,1517
Islam	None of you believers until he loves for his brother what he loves for himself. – Sunnah, Bukhari and Muslim
Jainism	A man should wander about treating all creatures and he himself would be treated. – Sutrakritanga 1.11.33
Judaism	What is hateful to you, do not do to your fellowman. This is the entire Law; all the rest is commentary. – Talmud, Shabbat 3id
Sikhism	As thou deemest thyself, so deem others. I am a stranger to no one; and no one is a stranger to me. Indeed, I am a friend to all. – Guru Granth Sahib
Taoism	Regard your neighbor's gain as your gain, and your neighbor's loss as your own loss. – Tai Shang Kan Yin P'ien
Zoroastrianism	That nature alone is good which refrains from doing another whatsoever is not good for itself. – Dadisten-l-dinik, 94.5

The Golden Rule can also be explained from the perspectives of psychology, philosophy, sociology, human evolution, and economics.

Psychologically, it involves a person empathising with others.

Philosophically, it involves a person perceiving their neighbour also as "I" or "self".

Sociologically, "love your neighbour as yourself" is applicable between individuals, between groups, and also between individuals and groups.

Evolution – "reciprocal altruism" is seen as a distinctive advance in the capacity of human groups to survive and reproduce, as their exceptional brains

Religion, Beliefs 41

Figure 3.1 The Golden Rule

demanded exceptionally long childhoods and ongoing provision and protection even beyond that of the immediate family.

Economics – Richard Swift, referring to ideas from David Graeber, suggests that "without some kind of reciprocity society would no longer be able to exist".[10]

It is also important to acknowledge that the Golden Rule has been adopted as a global ethic and does not belong to any one religion. Several humanist organisations recognise the Golden Rule as not requiring a religious conviction, and some will attest that not a single one of the versions of the Golden Rule requires a belief in God.

The Spirit

The spirit or soul with its immaterial and unknowable qualities is more difficult to incorporate in any "scientific" system.

The Oxford English Dictionary[11] gives "spirit" four pages and twenty-four sub-sections including "the animating or vital principles in man", "the soul of a person as commended by God", "active or essential principle or power of some emotion or state of mind", "subtle or intangible element or principle in material things". It may still not be clear from these definitions how the spirit of a person is separate from his mental state, and the nearest it may be possible to arrive at for a convinced materialist is that the spirit, like the wind, is a force you cannot see but know by its effects.

42   *Religion, Beliefs*

The following are some of the more common attempts to define what is spirit:

What is Spirit?

• Immaterial part of man	• Inspired
• Religion/beliefs/conviction	• Emotional calmness
• Soul - vitality	• Everyday ecstasy
• Quintessence of various forms	• Sense of harmony
• Life force	• Sense of belonging
• Breath of life	• Knowing sure from within
• A possession	• Transcendent force
• Something higher	• Mystical experience

Figure 3.2 What Is Spirit?

Spiritual Practice

It is the link with "special states of consciousness" and the spiritual practices of prayer, meditation, contemplation, that have drawn millions of people back to some form of "spiritual practice". And it is the assumed link with positive health, a "sense of wellbeing", "inner peace", "harmony", "balance" that has seen the growth of the consciousness therapies. By transforming one's consciousness it is believed that unwanted, unpleasant and unhealthy aspects of behaviour and emotions can be altered. Nearly all of the newer psychotherapies – mind-body therapies and humanistic therapies – work on the assumption that healing involves an alteration in consciousness and the development of awareness. "Becoming aware" and "maximising one's potential" are the buzz words of the growth movement that arose during the sixties and that form part of modern secular spiritual practice. It is easy to dismiss many of these approaches to healthcare as signs of the narcissistic-culture and self-absorption linked to Western affluence. However, the end-point to many of these practices appears to be remarkably similar, and secular descriptions of these states of consciousness are almost identical to those found in Buddhist, Christian and Jewish literature. They have been described by poets and writers throughout time. They have in common elements which lift them out of ordinary emotional experiences one may have on a day-to-day basis. Their extraordinariness is often startling and for many may mark the beginning of profound changes, psychological as well as physical.

Lines composed a few miles above Tintern Abbey, on revising the Banks of the Wye during a Tour. July 13, 1798

*. . . that serene and blessed mood
in which the affections gently lead us on, –
until the breath of this corporeal frame*

and even the motion of our human blood
almost suspended, we are laid asleep
in body, and become a living soul;
while with any eye made quiet by the power
of harmony, and deep power of joy,
we see into the life of things.

William Wordsworth[12]

The thing happened one summer afternoon, on the school cricket field, while I was sitting on the grass, waiting my turn to bat. I was thinking about nothing in particular, merely enjoying the pleasures of midsummer idleness. Suddenly, and without warning, something invisible seemed to be drawn across the sky, transforming the world about me into a kind of tent of concentrated and enhanced significance. What had been merely an outside became an inside. The objective was somehow transformed into a completely subjective fact, which was experienced as mine, but on a level where the word had no meaning – for "I" was no longer the familiar ego. Nothing more can be said about the experience; it brought no accession of knowledge about anything except, very obscurely, the knower and his way of knowing. After a few minutes there was a "return to normalcy". The event made a deep impression on me at the time; but, because it did not fit into any of the thought patterns – religious, philosophical, scientific – with which, as a boy of fifteen, I was familiar, it came to seem more and more anomalous, more and more irrelevant to "real life", and was finally forgotten.

It is these observable and measurable changes that have allowed for the introduction of meditation (mindfulness) as a therapy into several orthodox medical centre. Meditation can be defined a state of "relaxed non-aroused physiological functioning" and the changes that have been identified with this state include:

1. Slowing of the pulse
2. Lowering of blood pressure
3. Reduction in breathing rate
4. Increase in blood flow to fingers and toes
5. Changes in oxygen and CO_2 concentrations in the blood
6. Reduction in lactate
7. Alterations in brainwave pattern: (a) increase in alpha brainwave activity (b) synchronisation of brainwaves (left and right hemispheres).

Some of these can be observed during the practice of meditation. Regular practice produces a "carry-over" effect which has proved effective in the management of several clinical disorders, including migraine, high blood pressure, sleep disturbance, pain relief, anxiety and other stress-related disorders. Far more commonly, however, is the use of meditation (mindfulness) as a spiritual exercise and a technique for cultivating compassion.

44 *Religion, Beliefs*

I finish this section with a series of brief observations that I try to use as guides whilst claiming not to be religious or attached to a religion.

Wise Guides and Wise Words

1. Three Wise Men and Three Wise Women

   Over the years I have allowed myself to be "adopted" by three "wise men" and three "wise women". They can be either dead or alive, and I give myself permission to change them along my journey. The following are current "holders" of this position:
   Men: Mahatma Gandhi, Rumi, Jeremy Holmes
   Women: Mary Wollstonecroft, Hannah Arendt, Greta Thunberg

2. Sayings I keep close to me

   - Retain a devotional attitude to mystery
   - You don't know, I don't know, and nobody knows
   - Learn to tolerate uncertainty
   - Follow the Golden Rule
   - An unexamined life is not worth living
   - Blessed are those who are tested
   - Be the things you wish to see
   - It is not religious business – it is human business
   - You and I have to live as if the you and the I do not exist
   - It is no measure of health to be well adjusted to a profoundly sick society
   - Anger turned within leads to depression
   - Anger turned sideways leads to wit
   - In times of havoc and crisis people turn to pied pipers – charismatic leaders like the Pied Piper of Hamelin. Those who follow him pay with the lives of their children
   - Expect and accept

Notes

1 Press and Information Office, Republic of Cyprus (2012). *The Latins of Cyprus.* Available at: https://doczz.net/doc/2633318/the-latins-of-cyprus–ministry-of-foreign-affairs. Last accessed: May 2022.
2 Press and Information Office, Republic of Cyprus (2012). *Ibid.*
3 W. James (1960. Originally published 1902). *The Varieties of Religious Experience: A Study in Human Nature.* Honley. Collins Fount Paperbacks.
4 C. Sharma (1960). *A Critical Survey of Indian Philosophy.* New Delhi. Motilal Banarsidass Publishing House.
5 L. Kolakowski (1982). *Religion.* Glasgow. Harper Collins.
6 R. M. Sapolsky (2017). *Behave: The Biology of Humans at Our Best and Worst.* London. Bodley Head.

Religion, Beliefs 45

7 P. Pietroni (2020). *Poetry of Morality, The Religions, and Compassion*. Albuquerque. Fresco Books.
8 A. Flew (Ed.) (1979). *Dictionary of Philosophy (Pan Reference Books)*. London. Macmillan Publishers.
9 J. A. Wilson (1956). *The Culture of Ancient Egypt*. Chicago. University of Chicago.
10 R. Swift (2015). Pathways & Possibilities. *New Internationalist*. July. Available at: https://digital.newint.com.au/issues/102/articles/2351?msclkid=a433a33fcebc11ec8 327df3d335482ab. Last accessed: May 2022.
11 *Oxford English Dictionary* (1989, originally published 1884). Oxford. Oxford University Press.
12 W. Wordsworth (1798). *Lines Composed a Few Miles Above Tintern Abbey, on Revisiting the Banks of the Wye During a Tour*. Available at: www.poetryfoundation.org/poems/45527/lines-composed-a-few-miles-above-tintern-abbey-on-revisiting-the-banks-of-the-wye-during-a-tour-july-13–1798?msclkid=aad98606ced911ecb258d66 e3a189bb7. Last accessed: May 2022.

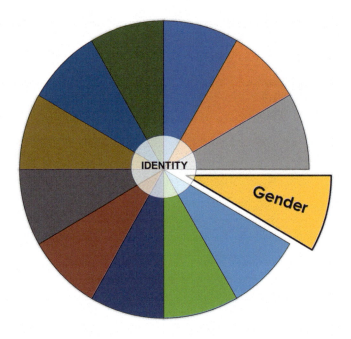

Figure 4.0

4 Gender, Gender Role, Genetics

Figure 4.0

Section 1: Biography

This particular chapter engages with some of the most current and most controversial issues regarding identity. The mixture of biology and genetics, culture and society, psychology and surgery gender realignment, and the legal consequences all impinge on identity and all have changed within the last 20–30 years. I will start with my own personal journey as it impinged on me, my family, and my professional engagement with these complex and heavily politicised issues.

Story 1

My youngest son married a fellow student at Oxford and is offered a sabbatical at Harvard for two years. He is about to leave the UK with wife and two boys aged six and two. He phones me and asks to come and discuss something important. I, assuming he wants to top up his scholarship, prepared to say "of course". The conversation is roughly as follows:

Son: Dad, you need to know that A (his wife) has decided to come out as gay.
Me: Oh, I am so sorry for you. It must be so difficult for you.
Son: No Dad, I haven't finished. I have also decided to come out and we are both going to Harvard as a gay couple.
Me: Now, very confused and knows he is likely to say the wrong thing, let alone ask the question he would like to ask.

Story 2

For some years after they returned from Harvard, I would pick up my two grandchildren from school once a week to allow the parents to work later than usual.

DOI: 10.4324/9781003401414-5

48 *Gender, Gender Role, Genetics*

The eldest (14/15) would sit in the front of the car and his younger brother (10/11) in the back. The conversation went as follows:

Me: *B* (eldest), *do you have a girlfriend?*
B: *Grandad, don't you know I am "bi"?*
C: (Younger brother in the back) *Grandad, I want you to know I am heterosexual.*
Me: Grandad by this time knows he is out of his depths and concentrates on getting his two grandchildren safely home and does not raise the subject again.

Story 3

Son and daughter in-law live together for about six years after returning from the States, agree to divorce and now married to same-sex partners. Both grandsons now 19 and 17 happily residing in their own sexual identity and co-habiting alternate weeks with their parents.

Story 4

Back to the beginning.

Born in Cyprus in 1942, the possibility of stories one to three occurring would have been impossible. One of my own early memories: I was 10 or 11, and well before puberty was when a male friend of my parents reached out and grabbed my testicles, saying he was checking that they were getting bigger.

Deprived of any discussion or education re: sexual matters, and not having a sister, the usual, "I will show you mine, if you show me yours" was never possible. As mentioned in Chapter 3 – Religions, the Roman Catholic probation on masturbation and "self-abuse" ensured that sexual activity and thoughts of any kind was followed by guilt and self-loathing. However, my pubertal sexual drive and the presence of two young Turkish maids gave me the occasional opportunity to observe them semi-naked.

Story 5

I became increasingly concerned regarding penis size. Exploring my father's examination cupboard, I saw what I took to be a condom, and attempted to place it on my penis. It proved to be impossible, which reassured me that I must be adequately provided. After further attempts I realised it was not a condom, but a finger-cot for doing rectal examinations.

Story 6

I read Alberto Moravia, "*Woman from Rome*"[1] and my pursuit of pornographic magazines and books were a steady accompaniment of my early and mid-teens.

Aged 17, I joined a close friend who suggested we visited the red-light district not far from our home and within sight of the Roman Catholic Church. He knocked on the door and disappeared inside. I hearing the chime of the church bells turned round and fled from this attempt at "doing it". In fact, when I married my fellow student aged 22, we were both virgins.

Story 7

At medical school in the early sixties, homosexuality was still not only a crime, but considered a mental, physical and moral disorder. Some homosexuals were referred for psychiatric treatment. This included the use of electro-convulsive treatment (ECT) and I, as a medical student, observed this horrific procedure being employed on a boy/man younger than me.

Story 8

I practiced as a general practitioner (family doctor) in London for over 25 years during the emerging AIDS epidemic. I saw many gay men as patients and many of them referred their partners and friends to me. I felt quite at ease providing them with the support they needed. On one occasion one of the more "dramatic" gay men arrived with two tickets for the opera to see Don Giovani at Covent Garden. My only embarrassment was when he stood up in his sky-blue suit to cheer Rugero Raimonde at the end of one of his amazing renditions. He informed me later that this 6 ft 3 inch hulk of a man was both gay and gentle – a big "poofter" – his words, not mine. It is one of the great privileges of being a family doctor, how much you learn from your own patients. I will expand on my own relationship with homosexuality in the final section of the chapter.

Story 9

When I finished my training as a Jungian analyst, I was asked to teach on the student course. One of my series of seminars was on gender, sex and sexuality. I draw on this work in the following section.

Section 2: Literature Overview

Disentangling the various and extensive streams of thought and scholarship that impinge on the topic of gender/gender role and gender attribution would require as many books as there are chapters in this book. Re-reading my own lectures on this topic over the last 15 years, I realise now how out-of-date they may appear. The last ten years of the "wars of gender attribution" the use of hormonal and surgical reconstruction have politicised this area of work. There is currently an ongoing legal case against the Gender Unit at the Tavistock Clinic in London.

50 *Gender, Gender Role, Genetics*

I will limit myself to four major areas:

1. Biology and Gender
2. Culture and Social
3. Psychology and Psychiatry (including psychoanalysis)
4. Political and Power Issues (toxic masculinity)

Biology and Gender

One would imagine there would be general agreement regarding the "science" of sexual difference – not so. There is agreement that males have an XY chromosol pattern and females have an XX. In fact, all early infants have XX pattern which changes to XY after the production of testosterone. Occasionally, things go amiss and X) leads to Turners Syndrome and XXX leads to Kleinfelter Syndrome.

Similarly, the use of brain scans and electroencephalography has led to an understanding of right brain/left brain division of function. Male brains are 14% bigger than female brains (Aristotle thought this was because the male brain had access to semen). There is now general agreement that the epigenetic factors have a much bigger influence on brain function than was once understood. The strict biological model that I was taught is no longer held as an accurate explanation. This is very well outlined in Cordelia Fine's book, *"Delusions of Gender: How our Minds, Society, and Neurosexism Create Differences"*.[2] Carol Tavris summarises this book in *Social Studies:*

> Wandering wombs, an anatomically conferred destiny of penis envy and masochism, smaller brains, smaller frontal lobes, larger frontal lobes, right-hemisphere dominance, cross-hemisphere interaction, too much oestrogen, not enough testosterone – all have been invoked to explain why women are intellectually inferior to men, more emotional, less logical, better at asking for directions, worse at map reading, hopeless at maths and science, and ever so much better suited to jobs involving finger dexterity, nappies and dishes. Today we look back with amusement at the efforts of nineteenth-century scientists to weigh, cut, split or dissect brains in their pursuit of finding the precise anatomical reason for female inferiority. How much more scientific and unbiased we are today, we think, with our PET scans and fMRIs and sophisticated measurements of hormone levels. Today's scientists would never commit such a methodological faux pas as failing to have a control group or knowing the sex of the brain they are dissecting – would they? Brain scans don't lie – do they?
>
> Well, yes, they would and they do. As Cordelia Fine documents in Delusions of Gender, researchers change their focus, technology marches on, but sexism is eternal. Its latest incarnation is what she calls "neurosexism",

sexist bias disguised in the "neuroscientific finery" of claims about neurons, brains, hormones. Fine was spurred to write her critique, she says, when she found her son's kindergarten teacher reading a book that claimed a young boy's brain was incapable of forging the connection between emotion and language. The result of Fine's irritation is a witty and meticulously researched expose of the sloppy studies that pass for scientific evidence in so many of today's best-selling books on sex differences, notably Louann Brizendine's "The Female Brain", Simon Baron-Cohen's "The Essential Difference", Michael Gurian's "What Could He Be Thinking?" and similar books published by his Gurian Institute. Other popular books about leadership, marital problems, parenting and education likewise claim that males and females are hard-wired to misunderstand each other, to have different interests and skills, to learn differently, and to differ in empathy, logic and the ability to see forests or trees.[3]

Cultural and Social – Gender Role and Gender Attributes

In my own lifetime, the emergence of the feminist movement and feminism in the areas outlined have challenged and radically changed the stereotypical form within the male/female. Gender attributes were recognised.

If I were delivering the talk today, I would be wary about showing these slides. As with the Black Lives Matter movement, feminism has also taken a more deconstructed approach to the concepts of gender attributes. Those depicted in the slides were determined by men and are in effect the result of the male gaze.

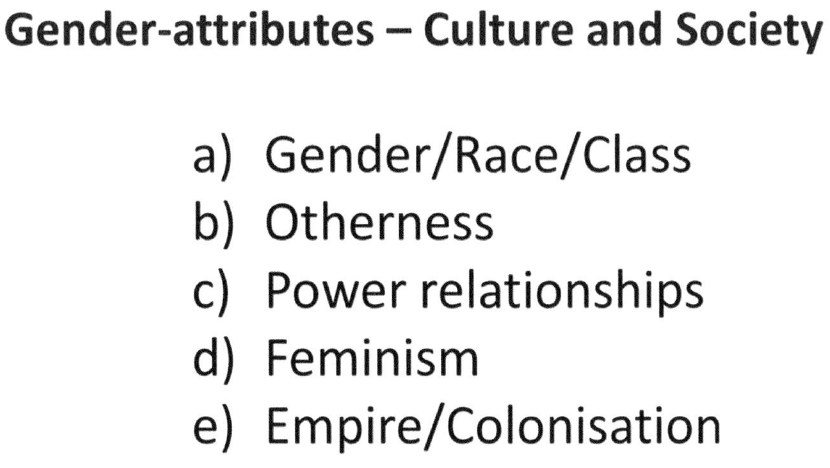

Gender-attributes – Culture and Society

a) Gender/Race/Class
b) Otherness
c) Power relationships
d) Feminism
e) Empire/Colonisation

Figure 4.1 Gender-attributes – Culture and Society

52 *Gender, Gender Role, Genetics*

The power relationships between men and women have meant that for centuries women have been trapped and colonised by the male gaze. This has led to the current belief that the root causes of homosexual activities are more driven by biology and genetics whereas lesbian activity is driven by social and cultural factors. It is important to remember that in many countries in the world both homosexual and lesbian life-styles are forbidden and illegal.

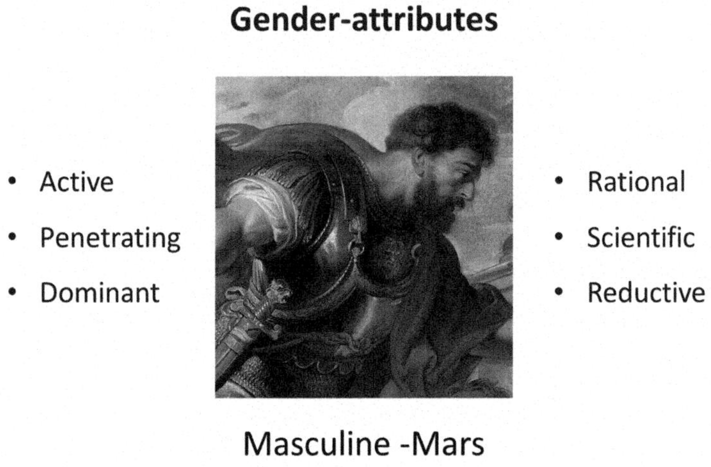

Gender-attributes

- Active
- Penetrating
- Dominant

- Rational
- Scientific
- Reductive

Masculine -Mars

Figure 4.2 Gender-attributes – Masculine Mars

Gender-attributes

- Receptive
- Reflective
- Containing

- Intuitive
- Integrative
- Holistic

Feminine - Venus

Figure 4.3 Gender-attributes – Feminine Venus

Psychology, Psychiatry and Psychoanalysis

Gender-identity - Psychoanalysis

a) Heterosexuality
b) Homosexuality
c) Lesbianism
d) Bisexuality
e) Transgender
f) Polymorphous perversion

Figure 4.4 Gender-identity

Psychoanalysis

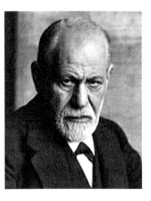

Freud

- Polymorphous perversion
- Drive theory
- Zonal theory
- Penis envy
- Castration complex
- Oedipal complex

Figure 4.5 Psychoanalysis – Freud

Psychoanalysis

Klein

- Object relationship
- Early oedipal
- Splitting/projection
- Sexual states of mind

Figure 4.6 Psychoanalysis – Klein

Psychoanalysis

Jung & Post Jungians

- Animus/Anima
- Logos/Eros
- Archetypes
- Theory of opposites
- Container/Contained

Figure 4.7 Psychoanalysis – Jung and Post Jungians

Psychoanalysis

Jung & Post Jungians

Animus

- Mind
- Intellect
- Thinking
- Linear
- Concrete

Anima

- Breath
- Soul
- Feeling
- Imagination
- Fantasy

Figure 4.8 Jung and Post Jungians

Psychoanalysis

Bowlby

- Attachment theory
- Secure attachment
- Urgent attachment
- Anxious attachment
- Angry attachment

Figure 4.9 Psychoanalysis – Bowlby

Psychoanalysis

Kristeva & Orbach

- Feminist reading not phallocentric
- Psychization of maternal object
- Bisexual model of adult love
- Language development and phallic phase

Figure 4.10 Psychoanalysis – Kristeva/Orbach

Gender Deconstruction

I illustrate this area that might also be called the "gender-wars" in order to indicate that at this stage of our understanding we are still at war!

Dr Az Hakeem, a consultant psychiatrist, writes in his paper on *Deconstructing Gender and Parallel Processes:*

- If gender = primarily product of society and NOT of the individual then . . .
- Is the wish to 'trans-gender' for the perceived benefit of the one's self or society?
- Analytic group = micro-societal context = ideal exploratory medium for Gender Identity Disorders
- Gender deconstruction enables patient to re-evaluate what it means, if anything at all, to be any gender, and to whom this meaning is directed through the group process
- If perceived relevance of gender is lessened from being paramount to inconsequential then gender-related psychopathology appear to lessen accordingly[4]

It is not surprising that what is now emerging from these gender debates is the issue of *toxic masculinity*.

Toxic Masculinity

As with much of the academic debates regarding gender, the concept of "toxic masculinity" is hotly disputed. The term itself was first used in the 1980s and was associated with the mythopoetic men's movement. This movement encouraged men to recover the link with the "natural world" – hug trees and discover their "feminine side". As with the discussions in the gender debates, toxic masculinity has four areas of exploration that include: biology; psychology; sociology and politics.

Biology

Is the behaviour of toxic masculinity (domination and devaluation of women, homophobia, wanton violence and the expectation that boys and men must be tough, daring and dominant) dependant on the testosterone level circulating in the male blood stream? This belief of "essentialist behaviour" is supported by the consequence of castration and removal of the testicles that produces "soft" eunuchs that have found employment in harems all over the world.

Psychology

Adam E Jukes in his book, "*Is there a Cure for Masculinity?*"

> takes as his starting point the belief that any theory of male individuation necessarily involves a deep narcissistic wound which results in an inescapable fear of dependency upon women and a terrible rage at the original maternal 'betrayal'. Men must, in the development of masculinity and male individuation, of necessity reject the mother to become separate individuals. They must also defend themselves against the 'feminine' and distance themselves from intimacy with women for the original betrayal, by maintaining power and control over them. The defensive structure which is created applies, by extension, to other men as well, albeit in a different form, essentially through the stereotypical male traits of aggression, rivalry, competitiveness and the acquisition of status and power.[5]

Simpson, in the article, "A Cure for Masculinity?" goes on to summarise Jukes' understanding of masculinity as follows:

> Masculinity is constructed out of phallic narcissistic defences against an underlying basic fault deriving from the loss of and separation from the maternal and primary object and it is formed in the crisis of the Oedipal complex.

> > 'Masculinity is not a crisis, but rather than masculinity is effectively a state of crisis, or a crisis management strategy, by virtue of its being effectively constructed on a structural fault.'

(p. 27)

58 *Gender, Gender Role, Genetics*

The significance of the Oedipal drama is that it elevates and affirms the significance of the penis in the emerging male psyche. It comes to symbolize all that masculinity is and should be. The relationship between the structural fault and the penis is what defines this book and the many expressions of masculinity Jukes meets in his clinical practice. The combination of a desire for the mother and a fear of the retaliating father is focussed around the penis. Examples abound of what men are prepared to do in order to pre-empt symbolic castration or regain their masculine status, providing evidence of the significance of shame in male psychology and the lengths to which men will go to avoid the evidence of shame and public humiliation. This feared collapse into failed phallic narcissism which is profoundly connected to the more basic narcissistic wound evokes the experience of being unlovable and intrinsically damaged or unworthy. As Jukes says, 'The penis is a rather insignificant piece of flesh, although it supports a mighty weight.' (p. 40)[6]

In summary, I would say that there is now general acceptance that the concept of toxic masculinity is real, and includes many of the following traits: risk taking; violence; need for emotional control; dominance; desire to win; pursuit of social status; the emphasis on toughness; dominance leading to sexual assault; rage and domestic violence.

Critics of the term "toxic masculinity" argue that the traits linked to the term are not inherently wrong or harmful and are often also linked to courage, leadership, bravery and self-reliance.

Where there is even less argument is whether the traits associated with toxic masculinity are the product of genetic, hormonal, biological or psychological factors or whether the social family cultural expectations of "what it is to be a man" result in learned behaviours passed from father to son, as in "boys will be boys".

I find the term "fragile masculinity" to be a more helpful concept and allows for the split between traditional accepted standards of masculinity and femininity to be not necessarily linked to gender i.e. we all can have both masculine and feminine traits.

Section 3: Linking Theory to Biography – Gender and Toxic Masculinity

As I look back on my own sexual development I become aware that much of the recent academic understanding applies to me.

1. Penis and penis envy over my development was always present, and soon to be 80 years old, I have made use of Viagra on several occasions.
2. Equally important, I recognise my yearning for feminine/maternal physical contact which is not linked to sexual activity.

3. I would definitely describe myself as a "breast man".
4. Underpinning and emerging as a response to items 1–3 is my own version of toxic masculinity:

   a. Competitive and desire to win
   b. Need for maternal contact leading to
   c. Emotional control and dominance of the feminine.

5. I have never gone so far as to be physically violent or undertaken sexual assault, and I don't think the term "fragile masculinity" quite describes my own gender attributes, but maybe I should not be the judge, especially as I profess to believe in, "I don't know; you don't know; nobody knows", or is this stance another defence against my unconscious bias?

Notes

1 A. Moravia (1957. Originally published 1947). *Woman from Rome*. London. Penguin.
2 C. Fine (2011). *Delusions of Gender: How our Minds, Society, and Neurosexism Create Differences*. London. W. W. Norton.
3 C. Tavris. *Social Studies. https://www.the-tls.co.uk/authors/carol-tavris/*
4 A. Hakeem (2010). Deconstructing Gender in Trans-Gender Identities. *The International Journal of Group Analysis* 43(2).
5 A. Jukes (2010). *Is There a Cure for Masculinity?* London. Free Association Books.
6 I. Simpson (2010). A Cure for Masculinity? *New Associations* 4. Autumn. p. 12.

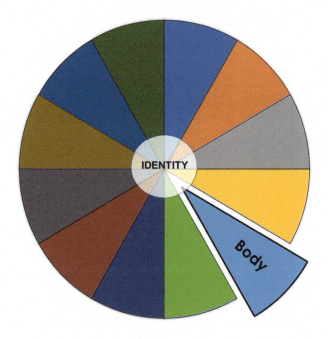

Figure 5.0

5 The Body, Body Type, Body Image

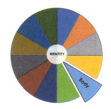

Figure 5.0

Section 1: Biography

Unlike the previous chapters on nationality, family and religion, the identity we derive from our bodies is very personal. In the chapter on genetics, biology and sexuality, we focussed on the most important factors that help to form our identity. In this chapter we cover some of the more detailed attributes and physical forms (hair; height; teeth; beard; nails; eyes, etc – the list is long) that help to shape our sense of self.

I start, as before, with a brief description of my own body parts that have been significant in helping to shape my relationship with my own body.

Height

As a pre-pubescent boy, my father was concerned at my slow development and I was told he considered giving me hormone treatment. I eventually reached the dizzy height of 5 feet 6 inches (truthfully, I never quite made 5 feet 6 inches). Sitting at our dining room table, my feet did not quite reach the floor and I remember the joy I felt when I no longer had to wear short trousers and, like my elder brothers, was able to wear long trousers. I suspect I would have been labelled as having a Napoleon complex or the short-man syndrome (the British who coined the term claim that Napoleon was 5 feet 2 inches, although the French insisted he was 5 feet 7 inches). Napoleon was often surrounded by his Imperial Guard, who were tall and wore helmets that accentuated his smaller height. Even to this day (I have shrunk to 5 feet 4 inches) I feel uncomfortable in hugging some of my young grandsons (some over 6 feet), as I only reach up to their nipples!

Hair

This is by far the most important body feature for the female sex, although baldness in men is now seriously treated with hair implants and shampoos that will sustain hair growth. I became "top of my head" bald by the time I was 30, but

DOI: 10.4324/9781003401414-6

62 *The Body, Body Type, Body Image*

have retained the sides of my scalp hair which only began to turn grey at 70 plus. Two of the political leaders of the US and UK (Trump and Johnson) are mostly caricatured by the style of their hair.

Beards

I grew a beard during the time I first went to the United States – I was 32. It coincided with the breakup of my first marriage. As I indicated in an earlier chapter, it felt as if I was going through a delayed adolescence, and was accompanied by attending "growth groups" and a ponytail. I have kept my beard and suspect this may have to do with one of many of the attributes attached to having a beard:

1. Secondary sexual characteristic
2. Signalling sexual maturity
3. Signalling dominance
4. Signalling adolescent rebelliousness
5. Signalling wisdom (philosopher's beard)
6. In my case, I dislike having to shave

Teeth

In Cyprus where I was born and brought up, the drinking water contained enough fluoride that protected against tooth-decay. It also left my teeth a dull shade of light brown. This never bothered me, until I started living in America where possessing shiny white teeth is clearly a mark of having achieved the "American Dream". It has taken many years of married life for my wife to give up hope that my teeth might become white.

Pipe Smoking

My father promised us all he would give us £200 if we had not smoked by the time we were 21. None of us did, although I stared to smoke a pipe in my mid-30s and still do. I was probably influenced by my father smoking a pipe and still possess and treasure the many pipes he owned. I thoroughly enjoy the whole ritual of smoking a pipe and understand its significance as part of my attachment-need i.e. it combines my need for a teddy bear, whilst at the same time allows me to associate with all the "wise men" who are known to have been pipe smokers. I join, amongst many others, Bertrand Russell, Charles Darwin, Harold Wilson, Johann Sebastian Bach. I do, however, connect my pipe-smoking to the link it has with upper middle-class English gentlemen, especially those in the Army/Navy/RAF e.g. Douglas Bader, Sherlock Holmes etc., and not to forget Che Guevara.

Strength, Sports and Athletic Pursuits

Although very keen to excel at sports, I was never very good. I did get into physical fights at school and on one occasion managed to overcome the class bully. Later on at senior school I won the boxing competition, but the reality does not reflect well on me. I let it be known that I was receiving lessons from the British Army boxing coach, and by pirouetting with fists held high, no one took me on (I have a picture to prove it). I think this must have been another example of my short-man syndrome. I did, however, from the age of 12/13 identify myself as an Arsenal supporter, which still remains as strong as it was so many years ago. Which team one supports is an important indicator of identity and tribal membership. The other sport I should mention is cricket; in my early teens, I became addicted to listening to Test Match Special (TMS), which is the live BBC programme on cricket matches between England, Australia, New Zealand, West Indies, South African and other countries in the then British Empire. I never played cricket, although because of my knowledge gained from listening avidly at TMS, I was made Captain of the cricket team at school (another example of my need to be seen as a loyal member of the British Empire, when Cyprus was a British Colony).

Food, Obesity, Body-Type and Clothing

Although it is true that young girls and mature woman both have a far more difficult and troubled relationship with their bodies and their clothing style, young boys and men increasingly have not dissimilar challenges.

Figure 5.1 "I have a picture to prove it"

64   *The Body, Body Type, Body Image*

At the time of puberty and teenage years, I and my elder brother purchased a chest enlarger. This was part of the Charles Atlas movement in the 50s and 60s, which, for us, did not last long.

Food: In our home was a mixture of French, Italian and Greek cuisine to which I added English (roast pork/lamb on Sundays) and later on Asian food, including curries (another signifier of the British Empire).

Clothing: These were definitely European in style, largely influenced again by the English class system (Saville Row suits – the last button of the waist coat always undone; classic blazer and cravat, and later on cuff-links). My favourite was the traditional British duffle coat.

It was made very clear to me that "clothes maketh the man" and that clothing style is an expression of the personal background, cultural influences and emotional state of the individual. Once I lost my need to appear British, it would be fair to say, I became scruffier in my choices.

Section 2

Languages of the Body

Before embarking on an examination of the detailed way in which the body has been studied, we need to ask ourselves: why now? What is it that we can understand about ourselves and our culture? The first British Medical Association (BMA)[1] report on alternative therapies identified touch as being one of the most important ingredients that seemed to link the diverse therapeutic interventions that were becoming so popular. This is not a sufficient explanation. It may be that we are witnessing something much more fundamental. Western culture, which has developed and dominated our world view for many hundreds of years, has required us to pay the price of separating the body from the mind. One of the consequences of this split has been our willingness to punish the body for its unruliness and instinctual life. Over the years, aided and abetted by religious, state medical and legal authorities, the body has been subjected to a level of control and censorship of which we are only dimly aware. We shall explore later the concepts of "having a body" and "being a body" but it would be fair to say that many, including ourselves, civilisation has meant the gradual taming of the body to the dictates of the mind.

It is becoming apparent that many people are no longer willing to pay the price demanded and are seeking a return into their bodies in a way that will allow them to keep their minds. Heinrichs writes,

Many people now-a-days believing it is high time they tried to save their own souls at least, all else apparently being lost, are turning more and more

The Body, Body Type, Body Image 65

resolutely to their bodies, massaging, feeding or dieting them with special care. In their bodies they seek salvation, life, meaning, refuge.[2]

This return to the body has its own price to pay, both literally as well as symbolically. In the United States, the price is astronomical: $33 billion a year diet industry, $20 billion cosmetic industry, $300 million cosmetic surgery, $7 billion pornographic[3] – all focussing on the body. These figures are over 30 years old now, clearly it is a lot higher now. Many would argue that the further we are alienated from "being a body", the more we will try to "have a body", and the body in question is one that conforms to the current perception of perfection and beauty. There are crucial gender issues in this search for the perfect body. Many of the casualties of the battle we see in our clinical work. The following figures may appear difficult to believe and are no doubt affected by the political correctness that has entered this debate. In the US, 150,000 women die of anorexia or bulimia a year, 5%-15% of hospitalised anorexics die in treatment, 40%-50% never completely recover.[4]

In the UK, there are said to be 6,000 new cases yearly, more than the total number of HIV and AIDS patients identified in the last ten years.[5] The average weight of anorexics is less than it was ten years ago and 25 years ago the average model weighed 8% less than the average woman; today she weighs 23% less.[6] The obsession for perfect bodies through diet, fitness programmes and cosmetic surgery is an indication of the importance we attach to possessing the body we do not seem to be able to reside in.

How then have we viewed this body? First and foremost, it is a structure. For most doctors, the study of the body begins with the corpse; the dissection occurs and the body is dismembered into its organs and tissues to be studied further under the microscope down to the cellular and molecular level. The body as a machine has become the metaphor for much of modern medicine and we are at the stage where spare parts surgery, from hips to knees, to kidneys to hearts, has become the major focus for medical research. The body is there to serve the person who inhabits it, and if part of it fails to function, we then replace it. We need to remember how recent this demystification of the body is, for in mediaeval times, dissection was forbidden, and Galen, that great physician of the Western world, was able to control almost 500 years of medical thinking with his view that the body was merely a vehicle for the soul, a kind of troublesome appendage. His knowledge of anatomy was derived from dissecting the pig, the dog and the Barbary ape. His description of bones and joints were of a high standard, but like his illustrious predecessors, Aristotle and Plato, he believed the mind resided in the heart (the Sumerians thought it resided in the liver). Modern day man and woman are not all that much better informed. In one study patients were asked to identify the site of their internal organs; of 720 responses, only 28% were correct.[7] The stomach was seen to occupy the whole of the abdominal cavity, the heart the whole of the thoracic cavity, two livers were marked and the kidneys were thought to be in the lower pelvic area. The way we perceive our bodies, both in terms of external and internal structures, are critical to our

66   *The Body, Body Type, Body Image*

understanding of health. The difficulties and problems arising from disorder of perception are of major significance to all therapists working with the body.

The language of anatomy and physiology has largely been a male-dominated activity, so that as Nemesius, Bishop of Emessa in Syria, around about the 4th Century, wrote, "*Women have the same genitalia as men except that theirs are inside the body and not outside it*".[8] Attitudes towards feminine aspects of bodily functioning from menstruating through to childbirth and more recently the menopause are all affected by the masculine lens that have been used to view women's bodies through the centuries. Two examples suffice, one from Hippocrates time,

> Women were of a colder and less active disposition than men, so that while men could sweat in order to remove the impurities from their blood, the colder dispositions of women did not allow them to be purified in that way. Females menstruated to rid their bodies of impurities.[9]

From a modern physiological approach,

> The sudden lack of these two hormones (oestrogen and progesterone) causes the blood vessels of the endometrium to become spastic so that blood flow to the surface layers of the endometrium almost of the endometrium almost ceases. As a result, much of the endometrial tissue dies and sloughs into the uterine cavity. Then, small amounts of blood ooze from the denuded endometrial wall, causing a blood loss of about 50 ml during the next few days. The sloughed endometrial tissue plus the blood and much serious exudate from the denuded uterine surface, all together called the menstruum, is gradually expelled by intermittent contractions of the uterine muscle for about 3 to 5 days. The process is called menstruation.[10]

But so far, I have described the body as if it were a static structure – bones, muscles, tendons, ligaments encased by a thin layer of skin in which several organ systems are located. The idea of the body as a living structure is one which orthodox medicine has largely ignored but which is fundamental to much of the work of osteopaths, chiropractors, and yoga teachers

To quote from the introduction to Ida Rolf's classic,

> As in all matter organised into biological units, there is a pattern, an order in human bodies. Humans can change towards orderliness, or they can change away from it. Human bodies do change . . . we do not mean deteriorate or age in the commonly accepted sense. We mean that bodies – average physical bodies of flesh and blood are an amazingly plastic media which can change quickly towards a structure that is more orderly and thus more economical in terms of energy.[11]

The Body, Body Type, Body Image 67

The idea of the body as a living system, comprehended as a whole, will lead us into the areas of study that are very rarely linked to the structural approaches. Blauckenberg provides one overview of this area when he lists the body as,

- The centre of orientation in our perception of the environment
- Focus of subjective experience
- Field of reference for subjective feelings
- Organ of expression
- Articulatory node between the self and the environment

When we approach the study of the body, what we learn from this phenomenological perspective is the importance that cultural and social attitudes play in the way we perceive and experience our bodies. Not many doctors would suggest to their patients that they may wish to consult a sociologist or social scientist because the problem they present with is best understood by that particular group of workers. This area of study is often identified as having begun with Darwin's *The Expression of the Emotions in Man and Animals*[12] and explores the body and its parts as organs of expressive communicational systems – non-verbal behaviour or body language, an area of great importance for all clinicians whatever their discipline but of specific and central importance to body workers.

Does body-build affect personality? Such questions have been asked by Hippocrates and Galen, commented on by Shakespeare, made relevant by Ketschmer's classic *Physique and Character*[13] and later by Sheldon's work on endomorphy, mesomorphy and ectomorphy[14]

It is the study of posture, gesture, facial expressions and para-language that has characterised the developments in non-verbal communication and that have enhanced our understanding of how the body is used to deliver messages to signal experience and contain emotions. Brown and Hall's work on proxemics behaviour,[15] or the study of the space and distance maintained between people, is of major importance. It is with the use and significance of touch and touching that much time will be spent on. We cannot understand the body as a whole if we do not study the importance of the skin as a separate organ in its own right. The skin is the borderline organ between the person and the environment and has both a structural function as well as a psychic one. To be in your body, you need to be touched. otherwise your experience of yourself is one of not having a body. The "touchy feely" impact of the growth movement has had a large influence in the renaissance of this area of work, but it is not without its dangers, especially when the cultural and transferential issues are ignored. Social touching is a culturally-based phenomenon and should not be confused with clinical touching. There are now excellent research studies identifying the limitations and dangers of clinical therapies that use touch as their major mode of therapy.

68 *The Body, Body Type, Body Image*

This concept of the subtle-body is found all over the world, but predominantly in the Eastern religions where it goes under several names. This energy is known as chi, prana, shakti and kundalini, and many elaborate systems of flow have been described to illustrate its effects. Hippocrates also believed in energetic flow which he called the enormon or physis – it later became known as the vital force, and for a while vitalism held sway in Western medicine but was swiftly banished with the advent of modern chemistry and physics. It is interesting to read a description of John Hunter (1728–1793), described as one of the greatest surgeons of all time, who still believed in the idea of the vital force,

> As with many others, despite the clarity of his thinking in some problems he also carried in his mind some useless lumber from the past, especially in the direction of vitalism that there is some special biological force as distinct from those of chemistry and physics. The fact that the great have weaknesses which all display in their humanity is endearing to those never likely to reach the peaks of eminence[16]

This useless lumber from the past has recently been reclaimed by many in the West, and the concepts in energy medicine have helped to link such diverse areas as kinesiology, acupuncture, Kirlian photography and spiritual healing.

Many who practise a form of energy medicine make claims to a scientific base and refer to the breakthrough in quantum mechanics and quantum physics as explanatory models. As quoted by Mendel, *"Physics, the most rational branch of modern science, has produced a sort of subtle body view of nature. Matter is both solid and formless energy"*.[17]

Many of the popular books on this subject do not stand up to serious critical enquiry. The concept of the subtle body is fundamental to an understanding of the symbolic and mythical modes of body experience and body embodiment, if I can use that rather clumsy expression. Jung's work on archetypes form the basis to much of this area of work, and Anita Greene, in a paper entitled *Giving the Body its Due*, writes, *"For Jung, matter, spirit, body, psyche, the intangible and the concrete were not split or disconnected but always remained interfused with each other"*.[18]

Jung's approach to active imagination, play therapy, painting and sculpture, dance therapy, the importance of alchemy and so on, all attest to the importance he placed on the body as symbol and the body as a somatic expression of unconscious forces – another way of expressing the subtle body.

Section 3

So, how do I view my body? How does it express who I am, and what is the identity it allows me to own?

Short, yes; hairy, yes; never going to be a successful athlete; poor at sports, so avoid them; not so good at dancing either.

Strong sexual desire, yes, and mostly not too bad a sexual partner.

BUT, I wish I were taller. I wish I could win prizes in sporting contests.

I cannot allow myself to get rid of my beard, much as my wife would like me to. I think I can dance, but actually, I can't.

So maybe I do suffer from the short-man syndrome, and that has been enhanced by a tendency to aggressive, competitive and toxic male attributes that only in my seventh decade am I prepared to acknowledge and address.

Notes

1 British Medical Association (1993). *Complementary Medicine: New Approaches to Good Practice*. Oxford. Oxford Paperback.
2 A. L. Heinrichs (2008). *The Afterlife of Images: Translating the Pathological Body Between China and the West*. London. Duke University Press.
3 N. Wolf (1991). *The Beauty Myth*. London. Vintage Books.
4 Wolf (1991). *Ibid*.
5 Wolf (1991). *Ibid*.
6 Wolf (1991). *Ibid*.
7 P. Pietroni (1994). *Languages of the Body*. London. University of Westminster Press.
8 E. Martin (1987). *The Women in the Body: A Cultural Analysis of Reproduction*. Boston. Beacon Press.
9 T. Laqueur (1986). Orgasm, Generation, and the Politics of Reproductive Biology. In *No. 14, the Making of the Modern Body: Sexuality and Society in the Nineteenth Century*. pp. 1–41. Berkeley. University of California Press. Spring.
10 Laqueur (1986). *Ibid*.
11 I. Rolf (1990). *Rolfing and Physical Reality*. Rochester. Healing Arts Press.
12 C. Darwin (1998. Originally published 1859). *The Expressions of the Emotions in Man and Animals*. Glasgow. Harper Collins.
13 E. Kretschmer (1999). *Physique and Character*. London. Abington.
14 W. H. Sheldon, S. S. Stevens, & W. B. Tucker (1940). *The Varieties of Human Physique*. New York. Harper.
15 N. Brown (2001). E. T. Hall (1966). Proxemic Theory. In *CSISS Classics. UC Santa Barbara: Center for Spatially Integrated Social Science*. Available at: https://escholarship.org/uc/item/4774h1rm. Last accessed: May 2022.
16 J. F. Palmer (Ed.) (2015). *The Works of John Hunter, F.R.S. (Vol 2)*. Cambridge University Press. Available at: https://doi.org/10.1017/CBO9781316034804. Last accessed: May 2022.
17 W. Bateson (2009). *Mendel's Principles of Heredity: A Defence, with a Translation of Mendel's Original Papers on Hybridisation*. Cambridge. Cambridge University Press.
18 A. Greene (1984). Giving the Body it's Due. *Quadrant* 17(2). pp. 9–24.

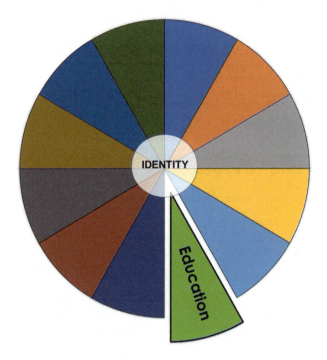

Figure 6.0

6 Education, Training, Learning

Figure 6.0

Section 1: Biography

I will attempt to describe aspects of my formal education (junior; secondary; medical). However, this will not cover the learning I absorbed through my work as a doctor/university professor, let alone the teachers I met on my journey, including my parents, my partners and my patients.

In the second section I will outline my own views regarding education generally, and I use Shakespeare's famous speech from *As You Like It: Act II, Scene VII – The Forest (All the World's a Stage)*.[1] I will introduce lines from this speech as I describe my own progress:

And one man in his time plays many parts,
His acts being seven ages. At first the infant,
Mewling and puking in the nurse's arms.[2]

My preschool memories consist of those I have been told, and as I describe in Chapter 2, my mother did not breastfeed me as she became severely depressed after my birth (I was not the daughter she longed to have).

There are photographs of my father playing with me, and I know two of my aunts helped to "mother" me. We lived opposite a small infant school run by the Roman Catholic nuns and I was sent there for a while, but was "expelled" for being too unruly. I did not become, as Shakespeare says,

And then the whining school-boy, with his satchel
And shining morning face, creeping like snail
Unwillingly to school.[3]

As this entry in the junior school magazine when I started aged six suggests (1949):

My estimation of my physical prowess was somewhat dented when I was chosen to play Tiny Tim in that year's performance of *A Christmas Carol*.

DOI: 10.4324/9781003401414-7

72 *Education, Training, Learning*

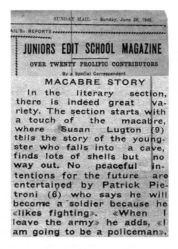

Figure 6.1 Junior School Magazine Entry

My early attempts at writing and drawings did not bode well for my future academic career. Most of my early school reports comment on my untidiness, carelessness and even in singing it was reported, *"Patrick sings with gusto, but cannot keep to the tune!"*

Three memories of my early school years I do remember were:

1. Fighting the local bully (my estimation – and beating him).
2. Plunging my hand down my teacher's shirt and not being punished for it.
3. Having to repeat a class year as my marks were well below average.

However, all this did not turn me into the *whining school boy* as described by Shakespeare because at the end of the term I (and I alone of my class mates) received an invitation from His Excellency the Governor and Lady Wright.

In 1956, aged 12, I left the junior school to attend the senior English School with a generous farewell from the headmaster.

Before describing my experience at the English School, I will try and sum up what I gained from my junior school experience.

Firstly, I learnt to speak and read English. We spoke French with my parents and Greek with our "servants", so learning English allowed me to start reading voraciously: Enid Blighton's *The Famous Five*, Richmal Crompton's *Just William* and many others. We all received pocket money on a monthly basis and I spent it buying *The Beano* and *The Dandy* comics and listening to the BBC World Service, where I learnt about football. I became an avid Arsenal fan and could not get enough John Arlott and *Test Match Special*. Those early years were the platform which propelled me to wish I were English and, like two of my best friends, to be sent to a public boarding school in England. The other major lesson

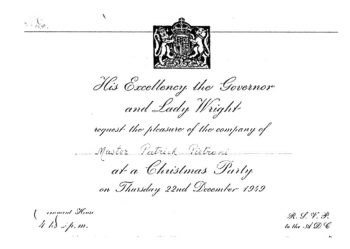

Figure 6.2 Invitation From His Excellency the Governor and Lady Wright

I learnt was that my two elder brothers were seen by the teachers, and mostly my father, as excellent students and the pressure on my future education increased as I had to meet their exam marks for all the subjects they took. One of my closest friends at the time, Haro Bedelian, went to the English School at the same time and for the next six years of our education we competed mercilessly and one or other of us were often top of the class in our examinations.

I (we) joined the English School aged 12/13 in 1955 which was also the beginning of the Greek Cypriot Independence struggle, which became an armed conflict with the UK military forces. The first incident I remember well was the burning down of the British Institute which housed an extensive library which had been the source of many of the books I had begun to devour.

The English School, when I attended, constituted of 80% Greek, 20% Turkish boys only. Those of us who were neither Greek nor Turkish (Armenian, Jewish, English, Latins – as we were designed) formed a small group of "others" who took Latin lessons when the Greek and Turkish boys had their own lessons in their own language. Some of the senior Greek students (17–18) joined the EOKA (Ethniki Organosis Kyprion Agoniston – National Organisation of Cypriot Fighters), which was the "terrorist" group that undertook the fighting for six years before the eventual independence of Cyprus in 1960 (still remaining in the Commonwealth).

An incident at school of great importance was when it was discovered that some of the 6th form Greek students were manufacturing bombs in the chemistry lab. The following day, we were paraded out in the quadrangle, and to our surprise and horror, we realised that some of the English teachers were in fact British Secret Service members. They appeared fully armed whilst a number of our Greek colleagues were arrested and removed. My

74 *Education, Training, Learning*

eldest brother's closest friend, who was pro-British, had himself become a special constable. He was assassinated (shot in the back) in the main shopping street, Ledra Street, which became known as the "murder mile". His body was brought to my father's medical office. Another incident occurred when returning to our home in the old part of Nicosia; I cycled into a riot, which was surrounded by the British Army who had sprayed the crowd with tear gas. I was arrested by the soldiers, and the following is a picture of me being searched by the British soldiers.

The previous paragraph is important for many reasons, and certainly has formed part of my education. At the time I attended at the English School, most everything we were taught in geography, history and politics was about England. We never had history lessons on Cyprus. We never were taught the wonderful fauna, flowers and birds of Cyprus, and I learnt more about the coal mines in Wales and the lakes in the Lake District than I did about the copper asbestos mines in Cyprus. I say this now, but at the time I was, and my family were, very much on the side of the British Colonial occupation of Cyprus, and we were lucky not to be ostracised, or worse, by our allegiance to the British Empire.

My eldest brother, who was a close friend of the young man who was shot in the back, has never stepped foot back in Cyprus, whereas I certainly have. The major informal education I have pursued is the history of the British Empire, its colonial wars and its complex legacy.

So, I left the English School having won the English spoken prize for reading, *The Traveller* by Walter de la Mare, and a good-enough report from my head master.

Figure 6.3 The Arrest (third person from left with watch on wrist)

Education, Training, Learning   75

My two elder brothers were, by this time, both medical students at Guy's Hospital in London, and my application to join them, although tense at the time, was a "formality". I was accepted on the basis that I came from a British Colony, and even though my "A" level exam results were poor – B, B and a C, I felt I had won the first prize in the lottery of life.

Medical School

I arrived in London in late September 1960 and started medical school in early October. Medical school in the sixties was not what it is today; the gender balance for one (over 50% of medical students entering training today are women). The practise of hospital medicine and teaching was all done by men. Each senior consultant led a "firm" of senior and junior qualified doctors to which eight to ten medical students were attached for up to six months. The first two years were mostly book work, lectures and dissections of cadavers. The next three years were "on the wards" attached to different consulting specialists e.g. cardiology, psychiatry, dermatology, gastroenterology etc. These two stages were labelled pre-clinical and clinical but were also known as pre-cynical and cynical. You took exams at the end of the first two years. 1st MB and final exams at the end of the clinical years, 2nd MB. You called your teachers "sir", and you dressed with shirt and tie (I was asked to leave the ward round with one consultant because I was wearing Hush Puppies).

The teaching in the first two years was through lectures and reading and dissecting the body. The teaching in the second three years was largely "on the ward", standing by the patient's bedside, or in small groups of eight to ten students. Once a month, your "firm" was responsible for admitting all new patients, and as a medical student you were expected to write up the case notes, examine the patient and present your assessment and diagnosis to the consultant on call. You were also expected to have examined the urine, sputum, faeces and done a blood count and test the sputum for the presence of tuberculosis (TB). It would be fair to say there were no "hours" you were expected to work and it was very rare for students to work less than 18 hours a day, seven days a week.

Consultant teaching varied from the inspirational to the bullying e.g.

Consultant	*Pietroni, what is your differential diagnosis of this patient?*
Pietroni	Silent and stumbles to reply.
Consultant	*Pietroni, say something, even if it is only to say, goodbye.*
Pietroni	Leaves the ward round.

On the other hand, I remember one of the older consultants who did ward rounds in formal dress, whispering to us before he started the ward round, to look at a young man visiting a young female patient who had a rare and disfiguring disease. He said, "*Never underestimate the importance of love in helping to heal the sick*".

76 *Education, Training, Learning*

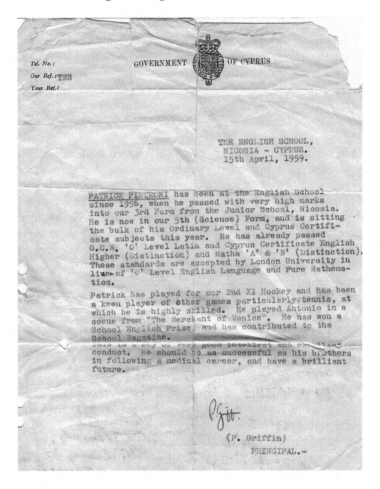

Figure 6.4 Principal's Report

There was more formal work expected during our time at medical school, and I did win the Golding Bird prize (scholarship and Gold Medal in Bacteriology). I also presented a paper on *"Dreams and Nightmares"* to the annual Physiology Society. Little did I know then that my readings on Freud would eventually lead to my training to become a Jungian analyst. I do believe we had an excellent medical education and left Guy's Hospital as a trained doctor able to do all three of the following:

1. Give an anaesthetic
2. Deliver a baby
3. Remove an appendix

I must add, of course, that I never had to do any of those three (thank goodness!).

At the end of our training, when we had passed our exams, we became doctors. A group of us from our year all went on a skiing holiday together, and after two weeks returned to the next stage of our training as fully-fledged doctors. We had each to apply for a "house job", which meant we were attached to two consultants for six months each as a houseman. There were only 12 such jobs available and to obtain one was to succeed in being selected as the "best of your year". It was also considered to be the first rung in the ladder for future promotion. The selection had occurred whilst we were away skiing, and I remember phoning my brother from the bus taking us to the hospital and found out I had been selected as one of the 12. My wife, also in our year, was also selected. We had the privilege of being the first married couple to be given a married apartment during our first year as housemen. At this point in our careers we were fully qualified doctors, and our future learning and education was obtained "on the job". I will continue to describe the next stage of our learning in the next chapter on work and professional development.

Section 2: The Academic Literature on Education and Training

I will address the first three of Shakespeare's *Seven Ages of Man*[4] and address the next stages in the chapter on work:

> *His acts being seven ages. At first the infant,*
> *Mewling and puking in the nurse's arms.*
> *And then the whining school-boy, with his satchel*
> *And shining morning face, creeping like snail*
> *Unwillingly to school. And then the lover,*
> *Sighing like furnace, with a woeful ballad*
> *Made to his mistress' eyebrow. Then a soldier,*
> *Full of strange oaths and bearded like the pard,*
> *Jealous in honour, sudden and quick in quarrel,*
> *Seeking the bubble reputation.*[5]

Firstly, I will say something regarding the importance of poetry in the educational life of the young learner:

Elena Aguilar, writing for the George Lucas Educational Foundation in 2013 explored the five reasons why we need poetry in schools:

1. Poetry helps us know each other and build community. Poetry allows children to put language to use to make it serve a deep internal purpose and to break rules along the way.
2. When read aloud, poetry is rhythm and music and sounds and beats – babies and preschoolers included may not understand all the words or meaning, but

78 *Education, Training, Learning*

they will feel the rhythms, get curious about what the sounds mean and perhaps want to create their own.

3. Poetry opens venues for speaking and listening and motivates reluctant writers.
4. Because poems defy rules they can be made accessible to English language learners and allows them to find ways of expressing their voices whilst being limited in their vocabulary.
5. Poetry fosters social and emotional learning. A well-crafted phrase or two in a poem can help us see an experience in an entirely new way.[6]

Emily Southerton (Director of The Poet Warriors Project) helps children write and publish poetry on tough issues they face, such as poverty, gangs and peer pressure. She writes:

Poetry ignites students to think about what it's like to share their opinion, be heard, and make a difference in their world. Students can let go of traditional writing rules with poetry. I tell the kids the most important thing about poetry is that people feel differently after reading it.[7]

Let's start with 0–5 years:

"Give me the first five years of a child's life and I will give you a saint or a devil"[8] is often attributed to Voltaire, who himself attributed it to Ignatus of Loyola, and was taken up by the Roman Catholic Church as its own dictum. There are now many scientific and research studies that support the statement.

At birth, a baby has more than 100 billion nerve cells. Brain growth and development by age five has reached 85% of the total brain growth. Learning requires the nerve cells or neurons to be connected together.

In the last decade or so, with the advent of neuro-imaging, we can observe how the mother's behaviour towards the baby's activities is of immense importance. The following three descriptions will help to explain how the capacity for empathetic responses (compassion) are developed and can be encouraged, making the mother or mother-substitute the earliest teacher/trainer/instructor for the baby's subsequent growth.

Attachment Theory

Attachment Theory was developed by John Bowlby, (1907–1990) a psychoanalyst, psychologist and psychiatrist working at the Tavistock Clinic in London. He started his life work before the Second World War, and his first responsibility was working with young boys who were separated from their families for petty crimes.

Bowlby's work differs in one central and crucial way from the work of many analytic theorists. It is not based solely on the retrospective formulation of clinical data but on observational data gathered in many different situations outside the analyst's room.

Education, Training, Learning 79

Mirror Neurons and Attachment

As the result of brain imaging technology, it has been possible to observe which parts of the brain "light up" when we are reading, having a conversation or listening to music. Studies of mothers breast feeding their babies have shown when the mother "mirrors" the babies face with smiles or gurgles, similar to those the baby makes i.e. mirrors the baby's behaviour, there exists "attunement between them". The hypothesis being that brain scans of both mother and baby would demonstrate the same part of the brain would light up. When the mother is inattentive or non-observing of the baby's face i.e. non-attuned, different parts of the brain light up.

During the first few years of life, the ability of a mother to be attuned to the needs of her infant is crucial to their development. This attunement is important to a child's ability to learn to regulate their nervous system and deal with distressing events. When a mother consistently fails to be attuned, different types of insecure attachment result. One could say that a mother's attunement is the building block to how one learns to be connected to others, build relationships, and feel safe in the world.

A definition of attunement:

> is a kinesthetic and emotional sensing of the other – knowing their rhythm, affect, and experience by metaphorically being in their skin, and going beyond empathy to create a two-person experience of unbroken feeling connectedness by providing a reciprocal affect and/or resonating response.[9]

Attunement allows us to respond with compassion to another's experience.

In summary, I would add that we now have the anthropological, the psychological (Bowlby), the biological (Lorenz), the scientific (neuro imagining) evidence to support the view that:

a. The first five years of an infant's experience are of major importance in the learning he/she achieves.
b. This learning involves language and emotional/relational cognitive skills.
c. The "mother" or substitute mother is the critical input into what the child learns, especially in the emotional education between five and 17/18 years of age.
d. Mindfulness training and helping the child to breathe slowly and deeply is now a much more common activity. Research has shown the marked benefits that can be achieved.

My friend and colleague, Maurice Irfan Coles, who sadly succumbed to Covid-19 in April 2020, has led the field in the UK and travelled over the globe giving seminars and workshops on his life's work of working towards the compassionate school (the title of his first book on this subject).[10] Together

80 *Education, Training, Learning*

with colleagues he has assembled the why, the what and the how to ensure the Golden Rule (treat others as you wish to be treated) can become a Golden Thread throughout a child's educational journey from the years of five to 17, ensuring that, unlike Shakespeare's description, this boy/girl is not the whining school-child, with his or her satchel and shining morning face, creeping like snail unwillingly to school. Coles went onto identify what a compassionate school would exhibit.

A compassionate school would exhibit all or some of the following characteristics. It would:

- have compassion as its key ongoing organizing principle, so that it permeates everything the school does
- ensure compassion infuse and enthuses its curriculum content and curricular processes
- ensure compassion forms the bedrock of initial teacher and continuing professional development
- have signed the Charter for Compassion with the Golden Rule as its heart, and with the Golden Thread pulsating through its arteries
- use the taxonomy of compassion "acts for love", as a key vehicle for both values transmission and as an audit tool
- have a complete workforce, including school governors and managers, who articulate the vision and live its principles
- have leaders, staff, parents and carers who model these values
- have a pupil population that aspires to these ideals, which will be clearly visible, both in their behaviours and in how they treat each other and adults in the school and beyond
- employ pupil, staff and whole-system assessments that do not undermine good practice but build upon it
- enjoy a culture of listening based upon empathetic understanding and a willingness to appreciate the view of the other
- teach pupils some knowledge of how the brain works so that they understand we are wired for compassion
- allow its pupils and staff the space to contemplate, to reflect, to be mindful
- be proactive in its local and wider community
- be proactive in building local, national and international cohesion
- be a health-promoting school that pays due regard to the social, emotional and spiritual aspect of learning
- be a school that really values educating the heart
- be a school that is culturally inclusive and meets the needs of its diverse pupil population
- be a school that safeguards its pupils and teaches them skills to live in this digital age
- practice restorative justice as part of its behaviour policy

Education, Training, Learning 81

- be a school that balances high attainment with his self-esteem
- be a campaigning school, championing the rights of others and the needs of the planet
- celebrate and regularly praise kindness and compassionate acts
- encourage the ideal of service, collegiality and love in action for our global interconnected universe
- be a happy school with lots of smiling faces.[11]

We can sum up the characteristics of the compassionate educator and the compassionate school as 'love in action'. The adoption of this principle in everything we do in school life provides the Golden Thread through which we help young people create a better and more just world. Students must still attain, must develop academic, vocational and social skills, but should have a more balanced purpose of elevating service, rather than self, as the key virtue. If pupils leave our care celebrating the maxim that 'universal compassion is the only guarantee of morality' (Schopenhauer, cited in Dossey, 2013:6), we will have gone some way to fulfilling our responsibilities to future generations.

Section 3: Putting Section 1 and 2 Together

Sounds, Music, Gazing and Touch

They say you learn it from your mother
That she will always be there for you
You, of course, know nothing of this
For your brain is not formed
For you to receive.

Yet, somehow you do know
You know in your body first
Then in your mind
At about six weeks you learn
To smile and to gurgle
No language yet, but you
Listen, look and feel
To sounds, to music, to gazing and touch
(yes and yes again).

You grow up, you marry
You have your own children
Don't preach to them.

You cannot teach what you have learnt
Remember what your mother did.

82 *Education, Training, Learning*

Sounds, music, gazing and touch
That is all you need
To help your children and yourself
To become compassionate
To others
It is sometimes called love.

Patrick Pietroni[12]

I wrote this poem in the midst of my exploration of how I came to understand my early 0–5 years and my early schooling 5–18. My mother was absent in the first few years of my existence, as I have previously explained. She desperately wanted her third child (me) to be a girl and retired to her room depressed and unavailable. My attachment history (à la Bowlby) was a mixture of my father (very active), two aunts (caring, but not physical) and one of our maids. I reported how I was sent home from my first preschool for misbehaving, and I suspect some attempt at inappropriate physical contact was the cause. This occurred also with my first school teacher and most actively with one of our maids when I pulled her upper garments down and saw a pair of breasts for the first time – I was seven years old.

So, it could be accepted that I suffered from an early attachment disorder, and developed an overly aggressive attachment response. And with my early (aged six) admission that "I like fighting", it can be safely assumed that my toxic masculinity responses in my later life were a continuation of my lack of experience of "safety", affectionate love and an unconscious need for acceptance. These deficits were further fuelled by my father's strict Edwardian disciplinary behaviour. In addition, being the third son I was in constant competition in meeting their exam results and achievements.

I fell desperately in love with my first girlfriend, aged 16, and I was devastated when she "jilted" me. I confess to also plunging my hand down her blouse, and wrote a grovelling letter of apology the following day.

So, I think I could safely acknowledge that my early years, 0–17, resulted in my developing a somewhat unpleasant personality, driven by unacknowledged need for love and a major maternal deficit. Aged nine, taken to the open-air cinema in Nicosia (Cyprus) by my favourite aunt to watch an old fashioned western, she discovered I had left my seat and got onto the stage of the theatre, pointing my fingers as if I had a gun, shouting, "kill, kill, kill" – that about says it all and sums it up! I continue my educational journey in Chapter 7 (Work, Professional Positions).

Notes

1 W. Shakespeare (1996). *The Complete Works of William Shakespeare (Special Editions)*. Ware. Wordsworth Editions.
2 Shakespeare (1996). *Ibid.*

Education, Training, Learning   83

3 Shakespeare (1996). *Ibid.*
4 Shakespeare (1996). *Ibid.*
5 Shakespeare (1996). *Ibid.*
6 E. Aguilar (2013). *Five Reasons Why We Need Poetry in Schools.* Available at www. edutopia.org/blog/five-reasons-poetry-needed-schools-elena-aguilar. Last accessed: June 2022.
7 *The Poet Warriors Project.* Available at: http://poetwarriorsproject.com. Last accessed June 2022.
8 Anon (2022). *Love-Money and Us.*
9 R. G. Erksine (1998). Attunement and Involvement: Therapeutic Responses to Relational Needs. *International Journal of Psychotherapy* 3(3). pp. 235–244.
10 M. I. Coles (Ed.) (2015). *Towards the Compassionate School: From Golden Rule to Golden Thread.* London. UCL Institute of Education Press.
11 Coles (Ed.) (2015). *Ibid.*
12 P. Pietroni (2020). *Poetry and the Education of Compassion.* Albuquerque. Fresco Books.

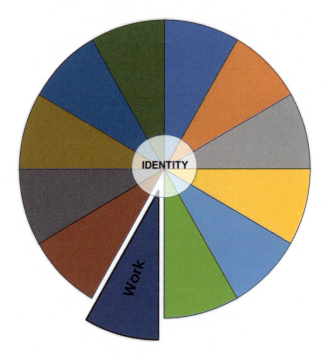

Figure 7.0

7 Work, Professional Positions

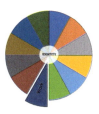

Figure 7.0

Section 1: Biography

Introduction

I have found it helpful to provide a truncated CV of my professional work as a doctor, tutor, academic, university professor, director of several charities and Jungian analyst, as set out hereafter. I will use this list to outline as best I can how my identity and sense of self (and the accumulated prizes and awards) have helped to shape my professional and personal identity. Along the way, I will include both positive and negative descriptions of my "identity" as judged by my colleagues, students and patients.

List of Job Titles and Professional Positions Held 1966–2021

1966–1967 House Physician, House Surgeon, Guy's Hospital
1967–1969 Medical Officer, Royal Army Medical Corps
1969–1970 Senior House Officer, General Medicine, Infectious Medicine, Hither Green Hospital
1970–1971 Senior House Officer, Paediatrics, West Middlesex Hospital
1971–2005 Principal, General Practice
1972–1976 Medical Officer, Royal Hospital & Home for Incurables, Putney
1974–1975 Visiting Assistant Professor in Family Medicine, Chapel Hill, North Carolina, USA
1976–1978 Honorary Senior Lecturer in General Practice, St. Mary's Hospital Medical School, London
1978–1980 Associate Professor in Family Medicine, University of Cincinnati, Ohio, USA
1981–1993 Senior Lecturer in General Practice, St. Mary's Hospital Medical School
1983–1985 Associate Adviser in General Practice, British Postgraduate Medical Federation, N.W. Thames Region

DOI: 10.4324/9781003401414-8

86 *Work, Professional Positions*

1985–1989 Senior Clinical Tutor, British Postgraduate Medical Federation
1993–1997 Professor and Director – Centre for Community Care & Primary Health – University of Westminster
1995–1996 Acting Regional Advisor North Thames (West)
1996–2001 Dean of Postgraduate Education, London University
2001–2004 Director, Regional Education Support Unit, Department of Health
2004–2012 Director, Institute for the Study of Cuba
2006 Visiting Professor – University of Surrey
2012–2017 Director, Centre for Psychological Therapies in Primary Care, University of Chester
2014–2019 Director, Elizabeth Bryan Foundation Trust
2017–2019 Director, Darwin International Institute for the Study of Compassion, University of Central Lancashire
2018- Director, Darwin International Institute for the Study of Compassion, University of New Mexico

Hospital Doctor Experience

1966–1967 House Physician, House Surgeon, Guy's Hospital
1969–1970 Senior House Officer, General Medicine, Infectious Diseases, Hither Green Hospital
1970–1971 Senior House Officer, Paediatrics, West Middlesex Hospital

The listed posts were considered "the normal" pathway once you had passed your final exam and qualified as a doctor. In these jobs, you were "attached" to a consultant and supervised by the senior registrar in the team. The fact that I obtained my first "house job" at Guy's Hospital was viewed by my fellow students, and of course, by myself, as equivalent as winning an Olympic medal. Whether it was the gold, silver or bronze would depend on how well you did in the job. I was attached to the consultant heart surgeon, and within two weeks of starting I was "helping" to open the chest wall and exposing the heart for the consultant to undertake the repair of the heart value.

The life of a junior hospital doctor in a London teaching hospital in the Sixties was full of paradoxes. One night I was helping a heart surgeon perform an emergency mechanical heart transplant on the floor, in a hospital ward behind closed curtains, to the consternation of a silent audience of wide-awake patients. The next night, with equal drama and the same amount of adrenalin flowing through my veins, I was listening to the Beatles, to the delight of a highly vocal audience. Both events were the forerunners of changes to come within medicine and society. The first, an example of the "hero in medicine" which laid the groundwork for the technological advances of live transplants, in-vitro fertilisation, genetic engineering and human embryo research. The second, an example of another

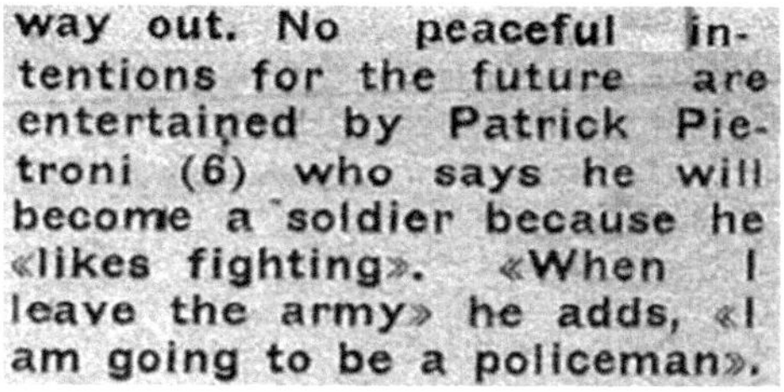

> way out. No peaceful in-
> tentions for the future are
> entertained by Patrick Pie-
> troni (6) who says he will
> become a soldier because he
> «likes fighting». «When I
> leave the army» he adds, «I
> am going to be a policeman».

Figure 7.1 When I Grow Up

form of breakthrough – that of music, ideas and feelings that were to "unite the world" around a pop group, and Bob Geldof, 25 years later.

It was, however, clear from the beginning of my first job that surgery was not for me.

My next two jobs were looking after children in a paediatric ward; the first at Hither Green was infectious disease, and the second at West Middlesex was general paediatrics. I enjoyed both these jobs much more; mostly because my consultants spent time with the junior doctors and demonstrated a level of care and compassion towards their young patients that my cardiac surgeon never did. I learnt how to kneel down to be at the same level as the youngster I was exam- ining. I learnt how to stay behind and make sure I saw the parents when they visited their child, and I did seriously think of combining the infectious disease knowledge with the paediatric knowledge and train to become a specialist in tropical medicine. I had, by this stage, got into the habit of creating in my mind "three wise men" (later I would add three wise women). One of the three wise men was Albert Schweitzer, and I began to see my future as working in a "Lam- boreni" hospital in Gabon. My having joined the Royal Army Medical Corps as a medical student had been predicted by me aged six, *"When I grow up I want to join the army because I like fighting"*.

Army Experience

1963–1966 Medical Cadet
1967–1969 Medical Officer, Royal Army Medical Corps

Looking back now the reasons for joining the army as a medical student seem clear and almost inevitable. The factors that ensured that this occurred, I can summarise to include:

1. Medical school fees paid and I received an allowance from the army
2. Following my father's footsteps, who himself joined the RAMC in 1940

88 *Work, Professional Positions*

3. My fellow medical student, whom I married in 1964, was the daughter of a vicar who himself had joined the army and was wounded as an army <u>chaplain</u>
4. Joining the British Army fulfilled my driven need to be accepted as English/ British

Following my house jobs 1966–7, I joined the six-month postgraduate medical officer's course which was partly held at the Royal Army Medical College at Millbank, London. There were about 20 or so fellow officers, and we attended a series of lectures and basic army training. We were given a list of civilian clothes were expected to buy, and the army tailor's provided us with the various uniforms a British Army officer was expected to have. We took an extensive series of examinations at the end of our course, and I surprised myself by winning a whole series of prizes and was first in order merit amongst my fellow officers. These included:

1. Montefiore Prize in Surgery
2. Tulloch Prize in Pathology
3. Parkes First in Army Health
4. Sydney Herbert First Order of Merit

On the strength of this success, I made an application to defer my active service by three months to enable me to attend the formal course to obtain the Diploma in Tropical Medicine and Health (DTM&H). My application was turned down after two interviews and I received this response from the commandant:

Captain Pietroni was again interviewed by me on 1 June 1967 at his request. He informed me that he had been in communication with the Secretary of the Examining Board who had given him to believe that the Board would probably accept him as eligible for the DTM&H examination in the circumstances if his case was supported by Commandant, RAM College. This has been confirmed by me in telephone conversation with the Secretary this morning.

This Officer's position is now coloured by the declaration of the Course exam results which were completed yesterday, when it was found that Captain Pietroni is first in order of merit – with 74% marks and first in both Military Medicine (81% – a distinguished pass mark) and first in Army Health (73%) out of 14 candidates.

In principle my personal opinion is still NOT in favour of acceding to this Officer's request, but, if this decision is reversed by you, Captain Pietroni should join No.82 Senior Course on 5 June or immediately after that date, if I am to have a fair case to put to the Examining Board.

This can be effected on receipt of telephonic instruction from you.

I believe, if I had been allowed to join the DTM&H course, I would have followed my ambition to specialise in tropical medicine.

Notwithstanding my disappointment, my first posting was at Shorncliffe Military Hospital in Folkestone. This had been an active hospital receiving overseas military casualties, but when I arrived I found it was a "holiday rest home" for Chelsea Pensioners from London. I was responsible for looking after 20–30 retired army veterans, all over the age of 70 (not that I had any experience in doing so). Nevertheless, I learnt much about each one and they were all keen to tell me their story. The only challenge that I found unable to address was their smuggling in much alcohol which was forbidden and which I sensibly ignored. I was there for only six months. We had bought a house and my wife gave birth to our daughter.

In my second year I was seconded to an army battalion as their medical officer and sent to Cyprus where they were to undertake training on counter-terrorism in the Troodos Mountains. I never understood why I was given this placement, given that I had been raised in Cyprus and knew the terrain well. We went "en famille" and I recall flying in an old Dakota aeroplane in full combat gear supplied with a pistol and followed by my family. We were there for three months and I had to rapidly learn my role and responsibility, which included looking after the morale and health of 700 soldiers. I did not do well when we were on a mountain exercise at night, where I fell asleep and was reprimanded by the Colonel of the battalion.

Returning to the UK, I applied for a posting to Zambia. Zambia, previously Northern Rhodesia, had accepted the offer of a British Army training team and I was to be seconded as medical officer to the 2nd Battalion of the Zambian Army, based in the North on the border with the Democratic Republic of the Congo and Nigeria. To the North we were in the midst of the Biafran War, and to the South Ian Smith had declared the Unilateral Declaration of Independence (UDI); Rhodesia (now Zimbabwe) was in conflict with the British Government.

I met, who was to become my best male friend for the next 30 years, Bernard Tanter, who was also a captain in the training team. He too had his family with him and we shared many holidays together with them. Bernard was an extraordinarily bright man and eventually left the army and became a senior language teacher at Winchester School. We became godparents to their children and he likewise became godfather to our second son Christopher.

I did finally enjoy my time in the army and learnt a very important lesson: how to get on with fellow officers you disagreed with politically. Most, if not all, the British officers were pro-Rhodesia, and at times, overtly prejudiced against the Black soldiers. I learnt later that I was described as a "communist" and the officers were warned not to fraternise with me.

Notwithstanding the label of "communist" being attached to me (no truth in it), a far more important event occurred that had a great influence on my attachment to being British.

The Biafran War was coming to an end and many Biafran military men sought refuge in Zambia. A Biafran medical officer who was a major in his own army was

90   *Work, Professional Positions*

attached to my medical centre. We got on very well from the start and it would be correct to say he was one of the brightest, most well-educated men I have ever met. I took him to the officers' mess (bar) for a drink and to introduce him to his fellow officers (all White). Over the bar was a picture of Queen Elizabeth II; he saw it, he climbed up on the bar and removed it, "*Zambia is an independent African nation and it should be a picture of your President (Kenneth Kaunda) that should be up there*". This caused great consternation amongst the White officers, and I intervened to avoid an ugly fight occurring. This episode was the beginning of my own transition regarding my need to be accepted as English/British. The Biafran major continued to create mayhem amongst the White officers by systematically bedding their wives and was eventually removed from his position to the battalion.

I also soon left my post and resigned from the British Army for family reasons; my father had had a second coronary and I flew back to the UK to see him. I applied for, and was granted, compassionate discharge, so I could undertake my father's locum in his general practice. Two months later we all flew back to London, and I started my career as a general practitioner.

General Practice Career

1970–1971 Senior House Officer, Paediatrics, West Middlesex Hospital
1971–2005 Principal, General Practice

My father had left Cyprus (where he had been in practice as a sole doctor generalist) in 1960. He opened his own general practice in the basement of our home in West London in 1963. Following his second heart attack, (1970) he returned from hospital and did not return to work for about six months. We returned from Zambia, bought a house close to my parents and the medical practice, and I started working as a general practitioner. The 60's and 70's were a golden age for general practice (family medicine, as it became called). The Royal College of General Practitioners (RCGP) was established by a group of both male and female doctors who established the academic framework and educational training for what was to become the specialism of generalism. I was fortunate enough to sit at the feet of some very special human beings (both male and female) who inspired me to the extent that after one year of doing my father's locum I had decided that general practice was to become my future work and life (and I have never regretted that decision).

I started work in the ground floor of my parent's home, with a waiting room and a consulting room, looking after 800 patients. By the time I left general practice in 2005, I had established the Marylebone Health Centre in Central London, a patient population of approximately 6,000 and a clinical and administrative staff of approximately 20 (some part-time only). I will describe briefly the sequence of progress and development.

Work, Professional Positions   91

Solo Practice

1971–1975 Principal, General Practice
1972–1976 Medical Officer, Royal Hospital & Home for Incurables, Putney

My wife joined me and took over the practice in Shepherds Bush, whilst I went back to hospital medicine (paediatrics).

New Practice Build

By 1972–1975 the practice population had expanded and we were able to secure funding to convert a vacant lot in a shopping centre just opposite the previous practice. This allowed us to have a waiting room, two consulting rooms, one nursing room and meeting space. This also allowed my father to return to work; for the next 2–3 years, my father, myself and my wife ran a practice which had rapidly expanded to 3,000 patients. I had been recruited by the RCGP to become a future trainer for those doctors seeking to become a general practitioner. I had obtained my postgraduate examination and become a member of the Royal College of General Practitioners (MRCGP), a member of the Royal College of Medicine (MRCP) and obtained a diploma in Child Health (DCH). The three books that became my bibles were:

1. The Doctor, his Patient, and his Illness *(1957) by Michael Balint*[1]
2. The Future General Practitioner – Learning and Teaching *(1972) RCGP*[2]
3. Inequalities in Health – The Black Report *(1982). Black et al.*[3]

I will list the other books that enabled me to continue my education. I stress, though, that I was fortunate enough and privileged to become a colleague and friend to several of the "Greats" in the formation of British General Practice. These included: Professor Denis Pereira Gray; John Horder; Paul Freeling, Sir Donal Irvine; Michael Marmot; Conrad Harris (who later gave me my first academic appointment – see the following).

In 1974 I applied successfully for a six month sabbatical to be attached to a new department of family medicine in Chapel Hill, USA. The then President, Jimmy Carter, was very keen to introduce the discipline of family medicine (general practice) into the American health care system. I was free to bring my wife and three children. I was 32 years old.

1974–1980 – Experience in Family Medicine, USA. My First and Second Secondment to the USA

We were due to fly to Chapel Hill in North Carolina in July 1974; in May that year my father had his third coronary and died a week later. We had appointed a

Figure 7.2 Marylebone Health Centre

full-time locum general practitioner to work at our practice whilst we were away and my younger brother, who had just qualified as a doctor himself, was also to work in the practice. It was not appropriate for both myself and my wife to be absent, however, so we decided that I would go on my own but that my wife and the children would come later for a long summer holiday.

1974 – July-December, USA Experience

My first visit to the United States was joyful, rewarding and helped to breakdown many aspects of my identity and personality. It also ended in personal calamity when I received a letter from my wife in mid-November that she did not want me to return to our home and would be seeking a divorce.

Let me deal with the months June to November first. I was made responsible for teaching the residents "the art of medicine" under the heading of *Behavioural and Social Medicine*. When I first arrived at the family practice clinic, I found the residents walking from cubicle to cubicle talking to and examining their patient/client who were already undressed. I closed down this model and changed each cubicle into a comfortable office where the patients/clients were welcomed by the resident fully clothed. During the course of the six months I was there I helped the residents understand and practice what I called "the art of the consultation". I used a video camera to show them interviewing their patients and found the responses from them to be "as if they had been given permission to act as an old-fashioned doctor". I think of all the accolades I have received, this is the feedback I treasure the most. One from a resident, the other from the head of family medicine, Robert Smith.

I can only add that receiving the letter from my wife seeking a divorce was partly mitigated by the response I received from the resident and the head of the department. I outline in greater detail how the remaining six weeks I had at Chapel Hill laid the groundwork for what I have labelled my "delayed adolescence" (see Chapter 4).

I returned to my home in London and agreed a quick and uncontested divorce. I returned to our general practice but felt the difficulties between myself and my soon-to-be ex-wife were incompatible with both of us working in the same practice. For the next year or so I took on a job as a general practitioner undertaking emergency night call visits to patient's homes. This enabled me to take my three children to school and be able to pick them up from school. I had, by then, grown a beard (which I still have) and allowed my hair to grow and wore a ponytail (which I do not still have). I bought my first pair of jeans and stopped sporting a tie. An incident that occurred in my bank illustrates how much this external change effected how my "identity" was perceived. Trying to draw out money from my bank, the teller did not recognise me as Dr Pietroni, pressed his buzzer below the counter; the bank doors closed and the police soon arrived to arrest me for impersonating Dr Pietroni. There was also the occasion when I had a formal complaint made against me following a visit to a middle-aged man who was complaining of abdominal pain. I visited him at 2:00 am in the morning and examined him and, fortunately, recorded all that he described and all the findings of my examination. I also arranged for him to be revisited the following morning. It turned out that he had had a heart attack and the complaint against me was that I had misdiagnosed him and that he should have been admitted to hospital. I presented my findings to a panel of three doctors, and it was agreed I had not been negligent, and that the atypical presentation of abdominal pain as opposed to chest pain, and my full examination was accepted as not evidence of medical incompetence. This was not only a traumatic experience

Figure 7.3 Feedback From a Resident

for me, but also assured me that my full and detailed notes are always essential, especially in the middle of the night.

I was now living on my own and divorced from my wife. At a friend's party I met my second wife (a psychotherapist at the Tavistock Clinic), and soon after we were living together and married in 1977. At the same time, I received a request from the University of Cincinnati to apply for the vacant post of resident and undergraduate director at the Family Medicine Department. This coincided with my second wife completing her psychotherapy training and we arrived together in July 1977 in Cincinnati, Ohio.

1978–1980 Associate Professor in Family Medicine, University of Cincinnati, Ohio, USA

My second episode of work in the USA; arriving in Cincinnati with my new wife and my three children certainly felt like turning a page, especially as my wife found out she was pregnant. Unfortunately, she had a miscarriage three weeks after moving into our new home. The Family Medicine Department was much larger than at Chapel Hill and I was given a full-time research assistant as it was expected that I would undertake a research project, as well as supervise the residents. The head of the department, Robert Smith, had been a senior academic primary care doctor in the UK and was incredibly supportive and welcoming. I decided to continue the work I had started in Chapel Hill and added to two existing consulting rooms a two-way window so we could observe the residents with their patients. I then obtained a series of TV cameras and began to study each consultation in great detail. The question I was researching was, "what constitutes an empathic and professional consultation? Why do some patients leave a doctor's office and say he/she really listened to me, or he/she never looked at me". Marie Marley PhD, my research assistant, was a music therapist as well, and at the end of my time in 1980 we published two papers on non-verbal communication and the medical interview. A summary of our work was published in *Language and Communication in General Practice* (1977).[4] In 1981 I published my first academic paper on *Community office experience for family medicine residents*.[5] My other, what I consider my major achievement, was to introduce Michael Balint's work on general practice to the American family physicians who were supervising the residents (trainees) in their own practices. Balint's impact on British general practice is remarkable, and his book, *The Doctor, his patient and the illness*[6] appears among the top ten, if not the top three, that all new entrants to general practice were expected to read. Alas, this is no longer the case. I was asked to write a paper for the British Journal of Psychiatry on the occasion of the anniversary of his book,[7] and I also described the work we undertook with the trainers in Cincinnati, *Training or treatment – a new approach*.[8] I believe the three years I spent at the University of Cincinnati laid the ground work for my future academic career. However, equally important was my involvement with my guru, Swami Rama at the Himalayan Institute. My wife, in the meantime, had joined an English literature course at the university which led her to obtain a Master's degree and to make a second career for herself.

We returned to the UK in 1980 having lived for over four months at the ashram (Himalayan Institute), and I was asked to apply for the senior lecturers post at St Mary's Hospital (London University) by the head of department, Professor Conrad Harris.

Academic Appointments and Experiences

1981–1993 Senior Lecturer in General Practice, St. Mary's Hospital Medical School

1983–1985 Associate Adviser in General Practice, British Postgraduate Medical Federation, N.W. Thames Region

1985–1989 Senior Clinical Tutor, British Postgraduate Medical Federation

1993–1997 Professor and Director – Centre for Community Care & Primary Health – University of Westminster

96 *Work, Professional Positions*

1995–1996 Acting Regional Advisor North Thames (West)
1996–2001 Dean of Postgraduate Education, London University
2001–2004 Director, Regional Education Support Unit, Department of Health

Between 1980 and 2004, I had a combination of academic appointments overseeing the educational requirements and training of both trainers in general practice, as well as young doctors training to become general practitioners. At the same time, I was still practising as a GP. I will pick out some of the highlights of these years:

1. Launched the British Holistic Medical Association and the Journal of Holistic Medicine.
2. Met with HRH The Prince of Wales, who later became Patron to our general practice – the Marylebone Health Centre.
3. Gave my inaugural professorial lecture at the University of Westminster in the presence of HRH The Prince of Wales and Minister of Health.
4. Raised over £6 million in research and educational grants.
5. Published three books (one with my son, Christopher Pietroni):

    • Holistic Living: a Guide to Self-Care – 1986[9]
    • The Greening of Medicine (forward by HRH The Prince of Wales) – 1990[10]
    • Innovation in Community Care and Primary Health: the Marylebone Experiment – 1996.[11]

6. 1996 – Led a consultancy team to Russia to help facilitate the transformation of the former USSR Health Care System.
7. Between 1978–2001- Led a delegation of 100+ GPs and department of health staff to Cuba to undertake bilateral exchanges of each other's countries unique health care systems. This culminated in the first ever meeting between the British Minister of Health and Cuban delegation in London.
8. Launched the Journal of Interprofessional Care.
9. Non-executive director of a property company specialising in the purchase of building and leasing primary care medical practices.

I summarised my professional life work as follows, "the understanding and facilitation of the complex nature of clinical, interprofessional, interagency and intersectoral work within healthcare systems".

It would not be right to omit those activities and episodes of my professional career which could be listed on the negative side of my professional career:

1. I had two further professional complaints made against me, where I was found to have endangered my patient's health:

    a. Giving antibiotics to a lady's infected swollen leg without taking a swab and identifying the bacteria.

b. Failing to visit an elderly patient with a stroke after a call from the family in the early morning (this was an administrative error as the details of the request were mislaid).
2. My junior partner in our practice decided he no longer wished to work at the Marylebone Health Centre. This involved criticism of my behaviour, and the occasional unwelcome letter, and we had to dissolve the partnership.
3. As Dean, I chose to withdraw the status of Trainer from two experienced GPs; one who was a close friend. They threatened to appeal and take me to court. This did not occur. However, many of the GPs in my "patch" felt I had been too heavy-handed.
4. I returned from holiday to be summoned to the senior manager of our local NHS board and accused of syphoning monies to my research project. As chair of the committee deciding on the allocation of funds, I was charged with fraudulent behaviour. The minutes of the meeting, when this decision was taken, were recovered and it was recorded that I had removed myself as chair and left the room whilst the decision was made. My solicitor requested a full apology, which was given.
5. I was accused by several colleagues, that as chair of the British Holistic Medical Association, I acted without due discussion; some colleagues resigned from the board.
6. Probably the one event I am most ashamed of is reducing a long-term administrative member of my team to tears –for a relatively minor mistake. She resigned soon after.

I have to acknowledge that some of my leadership failings arose form aspects of my personality that could easily be described as "toxic masculinity".

Figure 7.4 Retirement

98 *Work, Professional Positions*

Retirement and Return to Work

1996–2001 Dean of Postgraduate Education, London University
2001–2004 Director, Regional Education Support Unit, Department of Health

In 2001, the NHS underwent yet another reorganisation; my post as postgraduate Dean was to be amalgamated with another post, and I was given the choice of applying for the new post or take early retirement. I chose to apply and was not successful. At the same time, the post of chief medical officer for the NHS was advertised and again I chose to apply, and again, I was unsuccessful. I decided to take early retirement, and my wife and I sold our home in London (we kept a small flatlet). We left for our beautiful French farm house with 30 acres of land, horses, dogs, cats, hens, ducks, goats, a large swimming pool, a tennis court and above all, French wine, just 15 minutes away from Saint-Émilion and 30 minutes from Périgueux. We celebrated my 60th birthday and I became an avid farmer of an immensely productive garden. I expand on this time in the next chapter. I did, however, retain some of my visiting professor links and would return to the UK to undertake some teaching and lecturing activities.

My wife found living in France on her own, when I was teaching in the UK, difficult. In 2003/4 we returned to the UK and settled in a lovely home in Little Wenlock, Shropshire. We had always expected to retire in Shropshire as we had spent many wonderful holidays there when the children were young. By this time I had qualified as a psychoanalyst (Jungian), and we both started seeing clients at our home. Over the next two years we sold our home in France and brought over our four horses and two dogs (more on this in the Chapter 12!). I began involving myself in the local health and social care delivery system and was offered a part-time post of mental health director in the public health department of the Shropshire Council. This led to my applying for, and succeeding in, obtaining a five year funding grant to establish the Centre for Psychological Therapies in Primary Care (CPTPC). The unit eventually became linked to the University of Chester, and I was made a professor. The team expanded and we were fortunate to have two PhD scholars attached to CPTPC and were able to launch the Journal for Psychological Therapies in Primary Care. We focussed on monitoring and evaluating the implementation of CBT (Cognitive Behavioural Therapy) as the major available and funded psychological therapy in the NHS. Our unit and publications became quite controversial as we challenged the research findings published by the CBT proponents. It was at one of our annual conferences entitled "Mental health – how could we do better?" that we introduced the word "compassion".

Following this conference, we established a steering group of interested senior academics to explore the concept of "compassion", its rigour and relevance in our societies. This led to a launching conference and the establishment of the *Darwin Centre Trust* (DCT) and the *Darwin International Institute for the Study of Compassion* (DIISC).

DIISC was established in September 2015 to act as the operational wing of the newly formed DCT.

DIISC has four primary aims and functions:

1. to stimulate and organise exploration, research and education in and between a wide range of discourses and practices, as they help us understand compassion at individual, family, social, organisational, communal, intercultural and international levels;
2. to bring together these perspectives into dialogue, and mutual learning – promoting interdisciplinary collaboration and common purpose;
3. to understand the implications for all aspects of community life, such as education, health care, business, social policy, intercultural relations and so on;
4. to explore, develop and evaluate practices at any or all these levels and domains of life that promote and sustain compassion.

Three of the four previous initiatives, organisations, journals that have been initiated and established by me are still functioning under new leaderships.

Mentoring Programme

In 2014 I established the *Elizabeth Bryan Foundation Trust*, in memory of Dr Elizabeth Bryan, an eminent paediatrician. The aim of the Trust was, through the provision of a mentoring programme, to help restore and support the importance of care, concern and compassion in the delivery of health and social care within the UK.

A Working Definition of Mentoring

Personal support in the context of continuing education and professional development.

Key Principles
- Addressing current professional concerns.
- Providing space and time to reflect on and evaluate the professional task.
- Offering help with career appraisal and development.
- Exploring the professional personal/boundary.
- Mentoring is a confidential relationship.

100 *Work, Professional Positions*

Mentoring Programme Outline

The programme was available to all hospital and community trust, local authority organisations and general practices, and comprised of following stages:

- Meeting and presentation to executive board management or practice.
- Presentation lecture to staff.
- Potential mentors recruited from staff.
- Series of workshop training events.
- Successful training of a cadre of mentors.
- Staff and students requesting a mentor allocated to someone not of their discipline.
- Monthly supervision of mentors.

Evaluation of these programmes indicate that mentors value their experience as much, if not more than, the mentees do. Several mentors go onto to seek a mentor for themselves as indicated in the following exemplar.

Exemplar

A very senior nurse team-leader in her late fifties, herself a mentor, requested to meet with a mentor to explore her plans for retirement. She was much loved and respected by all her staff and felt conflicted and guilty at the prospect of leaving both her staff and patients. It transpired that her daughter had recently given birth to her first grandchild and she very much wanted to provide for her daughter and grandchild what she had provided at her work place for decades. This is only one brief exemplar of how senior staff find the conflict between how work responsibilities effect home-life and how home-life can affect work responsibilities. A few sessions with the mentor allowed her to arrive at a decision which met both her responsibilities.

The DIISC programme continues to this date, and I published a 10 booklet series on compassion that are now available in a box-set.

The Poetry of Compassion Book Series:[12]

1. The Poetry of Compassion
2. Poetry and the Science of Compassion
3. Poetry of Global Compassion
4. Poetry and the Education of Compassion
5. Poetry and the Psychology of Compassion
6. Poetry and the Evolution of Compassion
7. Poetry of Morality, the Religions and Compassion
8. Poetry of Economics, Politics and Compassion
9. Poetry of Leadership and Compassion
10. Poetry of Leadership and Compassion

Section 2: Academic Literature Regarding Work

I will limit myself to the two big areas of my professional working career:

1. Medicine and the healthcare service
2. University education and medical school training

Section 2A – Medicine and the Healthcare Service

From Professional Autonomy to Practitioner Accountability

a. We find ourselves in a rapidly changing world and yet, as a Society, we have done nothing. I repeat nothing, to meet these changes, to influence them or to adapt to them. That is not the reaction of a living organism but a moribund one. If our Society died of inertia it would only meet the fate it had invited. (John Bowlby, 1948)
b. There is no established institution, moreover, which now feels adequate to the challenges which confront it. (Donald Schon, 1970)
c. The 'Reflective Practitioner' delights in another's work and in connecting their own to it. (M. Kahn, 1977)[13]

These three quotations reflect the core of the critiques that will be found in the past 60 years of academic literature regarding the nature of professional practice and the relationship organisations have with the society of which they are a part. It is unfortunate that the aloofness and indifference which characterised the professional response to the changes in our society led to the imposition of a "managerial" and "consumerist" solution introduced by Margaret Thatcher. These changes which we have witnessed in the last forty years were already being debated by the Socialist Medical Practitioners in the early 70's.

The politicians of all parties were attempting to address the problem faced by society whilst professionals from teachers, architects, health and social care, lawyers and town planners attempt to retrain their centuries-old privileges of:

a. They alone determined who entered their professions,
b. Their use of expert knowledge as a tool to maintain a hierarchical power-relationship with their clients and
c. Their system of self-regulation with accountability only to their own professional group.

These three characteristics of the liberal-autonomy professionals were identified by Donald Schon in his Reith Lectures (1970) as being the rationale for this title *The Crisis of Confidence in Professional Knowledge*.[14] The solution to this crisis described and detailed by Schon and his fellow workers unfortunately did

102   *Work, Professional Positions*

not reach the ears of Margaret Thatcher. She called for Sir Roy Griffiths, chair of one of the leading supermarket chains. From the early 80's onward and the subsequent three prime ministers we have witnessed the emergence of managerialism, consumerism and the introduction of market forces in the organisation, delivery and regulation of professional services – whether in medicine, teaching, social work or psychotherapy. Harrison and Pollitt, in their excellent book entitled *Controlling Health Professionals* (1994),[15] track the emergence of the manager in the NHS in four distinct phases:

- The professional as autonomous
- The manager as administrator
- The manger as diplomat
- The manager as director

With the introduction of the manager came the accompanying processes of audit, clinical governance, resource allocation, targets and the external regulation. The professional was not only to lose professional autonomy but was to be made accountable to an outside body. More was to follow. Under John Major's government, the introduction of the Patients' Charger led to a host of other changes further developed by Tony Blair: *patient choice, patient partnership and the expert patient* programmes. We were now fully launched into the commodification of health care (physical, social and psychological). Managers were busily developing "products" and "packages" of "care" that the patient/client/consumer would choose from a "menu" of options delivered by professionals, ratified by "NICE", the carefully branded National Institute of Clinical Excellence, and put out to tender. A complete cultural change in health and care services had been accomplished and that radically changed the nature, language and context of professional activity of all kinds.

This nightmare scenario is clearly a caricature of how many doctors, nurses, social workers, counsellors and psychotherapists practice, but as the Bowlby quote (at the beginning of this section) suggests – our inertia and professional tribalism have resulted in potential loss of the core values of professional practice. We need now to return to Donald Schon's lifework to understand where we may have gone wrong and how we may retrieve something of these values form this continuing crisis.

Schon's seminal paper *The Crisis of Professional Knowledge and the Pursuit of an Epistemology of Practice* (1987)[16] attracted much attention to this concept of the "reflective practitioner", applicable in every area of professional activity. Schon called for the liberation of the professional from the tyranny of the university-based schools. He was challenging the influence of misplaced "scientific" methodologies. In his view, the university-based schools have succumbed to the erroneous view that good professional practice is dependent on the use of "*describable, testable, replicable techniques derived from scientific research based on knowledge that is objective, consensual cumulative and convergent*".[17] His different perspective involves practitioners *"making judgements of quality for which they cannot state adequate criteria, display skills for which they cannot describe procedures or rules"*.[18]

The writings of someone who described our current predicament, Sir Geoffrey Vickers (2001/1968), believed the assumptions underpinning the introduction of market mechanism in professional practice appeared to be that the automatic regulators of the market could substitute for the excruciatingly difficult choices posed by an ever-increasing demand pushing ever more strongly against a fixed resource which would otherwise fall to deliberate human agency. The tendency for Western societies to believe that automatic regulators can substitute for deliberate human regulations, based on ethical principles, derived largely, Vickers believed, from a change in what he called the appreciative setting, associated with the Enlightenment. It lay at the heart of what he believed to be the weakness of Western culture. Vickers was increasingly uncomfortable with the notion of causality as it is expressed in the traditional "scientific method" – how to connect elements known to be associated with one another in the correct way – when that correct way involves looking for a logical sequence of cause and effect. The billiard ball notion of causality, and the associated neglect of the impossibility of continuous linear development, has dominated Western scientific thought for the last 300 years. Vickers was critical of the dominant Western concept of man as goal-seeking rather than relationship-maintaining:

> The concept of goal-seeking, apt enough as a model of behaviour in those situations in which effort leads through successful achievement to rest, was generalised as the standard model of human "rational" behaviour, although most human regulative behaviour, as I shall try to show, is norm-seeking and, as such, cannot be resolved into goal-seeking, despite the common opinion the contrary.[19]

Section 2B: University Education and Medical School Training

I begin with a quote from Herbert McCabe, the Irish Dominican priest, theologian, and philosopher:

> We are not optimists; we do not present a lovely vision of the world which everyone is expected to fall in love with. We simply have, wherever we are, some small local task to do, on the side of justice for [our students].[20]

I will focus on the process and culture that universities need to adopt focussing on the relational aspect of their task. There is no getting away from the fact that

104 *Work, Professional Positions*

the primary task of a university is to deliver educational programmes that will ensure the students are:

1. Fit for the award (BSc/BA/MSc/MA/PhD/Dprof)
2. Fit to practice their chosen profession (to meet the appropriate professional standards)
3. Fit for purpose

In introducing the concept of "Fit for Purpose" I draw from a variety of the enormously rich and theoretically heterodox literature that is available.

Both Schon and Vickers were responding and reacting to the emergence of general systems theory. The logic of their critique was to call into question the traditional role of single-silo-faculties as the foundation for university teaching. Vickers wrote:

> In the last fifty years of the psycho-social sciences has widened almost as much as that of the physio-biological sciences. Further, and no less important, the studies of ecology and ethology have prepared our minds to think ecologically and ethologically about our own species. So, in seeking to define the field of a specialist in authority we have to ask, as we should not have had to ask fifty years ago, "Where does his/her discipline stop?"
>
> (Vickers, 1968)[21]

What Has Gone Wrong?

I summarise some of the main issues that have been identified and explored in the literature in the last five years.

Historical and Cultural

- The crisis in confidence in profession knowledge
- The move from professional autonomy to practitioner accountability
- The loss of deference to authority
- The rise and rise of consumerism
- The emergence of managerialism

Philosophical and Educational

- Those who can do, cannot teach
- The fault line in the enlightenment
- The tyranny of excellence
- The pure scientist versus the particular humanist
- Confusing training with education

Political and Economic

- The rise of tuition costs and student debt
- The conversion of polytechnics to universities
- The silo mentality of disciplines
- Commodification of modules and courses
- Technologically quantified outcomes
- Domination of research versus education

Career Paths and Employability

- The diminution of the humanities
- Linking excellence with salary potential
- Student enrolment figures and fees crisis
- The increasing mental health issues for students and faculty

Leadership and Change Management

- Universities as businesses
- 25% of academics not content with their salary
- 1 in 3 respondents felt their job was not secure
- Zero hours and fixed term contracts

A more thorough description and analysis is provided by the following reports, surveys and books (Gyimah, 2018;[22] Okanagan Charter, 2015;[23] Treadgold 2018; Watson, Hollister, Stroud & Babcock, 2011).[24]

Professor Mike Thomas, when Vice-Chancellor of the University of Central Lancashire, highlighted the challenges faced by organisational leaders who have the desire to influence changes within large organisations. He wrote in an online article (Thomas, 2018) for *Times Higher Education* entitled "Heroic Leadership is a Campus Villain" that:

> Universities are not capitalist enterprises, and leaders forget this at their peril. Business models purloined from the private sector will always be an uneasy fit. We occupy a distinctive position in society, straddling elements of the private, public and charitable spheres . . . rather than the heroic model, I'm an advocate of the "stewardship model". University leaders are "keepers of the flame", custodians of institutions that are more important than any one individual. During our tenure, we are charged with ensuring that our institutions continue to succeed in their remits to offer people the life-changing benefits of higher education and enable them to achieve their potential. These values are important because they provide the foundation of our activities.[25]

106 *Work, Professional Positions*

Steward and Stewardship

Steward is an old English word 12th Century – used to describe someone employed to "manage", or "look after" a large household. *Stewardship* has many theological and religious meanings, with links to the Bible and the concept of the good shepherd. *Steward and stewardship* is now in common use referring to environmental concerns, responsible use and protection of the natural environment through conservation and sustainable practices (Merriam Webster Dictionary). The concept of stewardship applied to higher education offers a way of understanding the entrepreneurial nature of universities, and in particular the relationship between education and health in relation to the development and "wellness" of communities (Callejo Perez & Ode, 2013).[26]

Stewardship and Leadership – A Whole University Approach

Professor Mark Dooris and his colleagues published a most scholarly and substantial report: *Healthy Universities: Whole University Leadership for Health, Wellbeing and Sustainability* (Dooris, Farrier, & Powell, 2018)[27] The report builds on the Okanagan Charter (2015) and provides all who are involved in this work a framework to implement the detailed recommendations and conclusions, outlined hereafter:

Recommendations for Senior Level Leaders

- Make a commitment to health and wellbeing a key strategic priority, acknowledging that this underpins core university business and productivity.
- Adopt a whole university approach. This means focusing on the entire university community; appreciating that health has multiple determinants and consequences embedding this commitment within and across all areas and activities; and connecting across boundaries.
- Ensure that action to protect and promote health and wellbeing is effectively jointed up with parallel agendas such as sustainability, resilience, equality and diversity.
- Balance top-down commitment to health and wellbeing with a distributed leadership model that embeds this commitment into multiple roles and responsibilities.
- Complement strategic leadership with a process of cultural change – building wide-ranging ownership and shifting mindsets among staff and students.
- Enable the development and coordination of the Healthy University through resourcing a dedicated post or team.
- Align whole university approaches advocated by different strategic agendas and respond to high-profile issues (e.g. mental health) within the context of a wider healthy universities commitment to health, wellbeing and sustainability.

Work, Professional Positions 107

The image shows how future vice-chancellors will need to understand that the concept of stewardship involves both top-down and bottom-up leadership skills.

The determination of future vice-chancellors to embed the concept of "alma mater studiorum", together with a university-wide (for faculty and students) mentoring programme will ensure their leadership is indeed that of a steward, and not just a chief-executive.

Section 3: Profession, Work and Linking Theory

In 2012, at the launch conference for The Centre for the Psychological Studies in Primary Care I gave a speech entitled, "Why are we here?",[28] subtitled, "When memory dies". The focus of the speech was to describe why I believed then and do so more now that our health service is in danger of developing organisational Alzheimer's.

I will address the question of "What is memory for?" in Chapter 10 (Psychology and Psychoanalysis), but I bring the chapter to an end with a trip down memory lane.

A Trip Down Memory Lane

I joined the NHS over 50 years ago, and the list that follows is how I remember the various shapes and changes it has gone through. Things were not necessarily

Figure 7.5 Leadership Styles

108 *Work, Professional Positions*

better in the "good old days", my memory is tinged with as much criticism as it is with nostalgia.

1948–1965 – Cradle to Grave

The first phase – "cradle to grave" grew out of the aftermath of the Second World War and was an attempt to provide "free healthcare for all at the point of need". The BMA opposed it and the compromises involved, allowing the general practitioners to retain a private and self-employed status, which they still do. Consultants had to have, as Aneurin Bevan wrote, "stuffed their mouths with gold". Doctors were in charge and for the next twenty or so years the hierarchy of the NHS was modelled on the military. We had medical officers of health, there was a medical superintendent in charge of hospitals and the consultant/registrar/houseman model resembled the army general/colonel/lieutenant. The ward rounds were inspection parades and the patients had to lie in bed neatly tucked up to be addressed by the general and the poor private students following the great men (for there were few if any women consultants at my time at medical school) were grilled and if found wanting were either humiliated or punished.

The metaphor of "war" still has a hold on medicine. We indeed talk about "the war against cancer", "the magic bullet", "stamping out infection", "killing the germs". In this phase the two other major professions, nursing and social work were still very much under the direction of the medical profession.

1965–1975 – Professional Tribal Warfare

The social changes occurring in the sixties began to disturb and eventually fragment this medical hegemony. Both the medical officer of health and medical superintendent roles were abolished. The Salmon report freed nurses from medical control.

Likewise, the Seebohm report allowed the Social Workers to become separate from the NHS and become part of the Local Authority. Even general practitioners who had been seen as those who had failed to become consultants declared UDI formed their own College under great protest from Lord Moran (Churchill's doctor and then President of the College of Physicians was heard to say, "over my dead body"). For the next ten or fifteen years, tribal warfare between these three professions produced a form of anarchy where consultants in the hospitals, still very much in charge of their own territory, retreated and took on a "bunker mentality" towards any change proposed by either the Labour or Conservative politicians who, understandably, were concerned with what to do about the NHS.

1975–1990 – Bring in the Managers

Several Labour Health Secretaries tried but were undermined by the doctors who refused to co-operate. It was not until Margaret Thatcher became Prime Minister that a serious (but misguided) series of changes occurred. She asked Sir Roy Griffiths, Chair of Sainsbury, to bring forward a new management system into the NHS and he, being an expert in supermarkets, presented Mrs Thatcher with a model of management that works superbly for supermarkets but is totally unsuitable for the complex human-service organisation that is the NHS. It is during the early eighties that we began to see the rise of audit cycles, "episodes of care" and even "care packages" – the introduction of IT, and the philosophy of, "what can't be counted, can't be managed". It is also during this decade that we see the arrival of death by a new project or report and the cycle of continuous change from Health Authorities, Family Health Service Authorities, Hospital Trusts, Strategic Health Authorities, Area Management Teams and so on.

One very important factor was overlooked: until now the NHS was consuming anything between 5% and 6% of GDP, whilst the European, Canadian and American Governments were spending nearer 8% of GDP on the NHS. The reality was that the NHS was grossly underfunded as well as being badly managed, and very little improvement occurred.

1990–1997 – Leave it to the Market

Margaret Thatcher's second term of office following the Falklands War saw her economic strategy develop into the model we know as Neo-Liberal. Central Control was not working, free markets were, and in the nineties we entered into our first phase of "market-forces" as the key driver not only to cost effectiveness but also to increased quality, and the balance of power for the first time in the NHS was moved from the secondary, Hospital Sector to the Primary Care Sector. The mantra and strategy became known as, "Primary Care Led". We began to see the operating of the Purchaser (Provider split), firstly General Practices became fundholding, then developed Multifunds, then Practice Based Commissioning. These were heady days for those of us in General Practice, but the tribal warfare between healthcare and social care now became fierce as budget skirmishes arose, known as the health bath/social bath battles. In fact, it became clear that "leaving it to the market" necessitated commercial confidentiality and undermined what little co-operation still existed between health and social care staff. The solution was to bring in:

1997–2006 – The Regulators

Tony Blair was in power by then. He abolished fund-holding and froze all expenditure for the NHS in the first two years of his government. We were still only spending 6.8% of GDP on the NHS whilst countries with equivalent economies were spending almost the agreed consensus figure of 10%.

The Audit Commission was given more powers. The Health Commission was established as an inspectorate, the Health Ombudsman was appointed and Professional Self-Regulation was slowly dismantled. There was talk of 'sacking'

110 *Work, Professional Positions*

the General Medical Council. Finally, the National Institute of Clinical Excellence was established as a sort of Supreme Court of decision making on clinical matters. "Evidence-based medicine" entered the lexicon and was seen as the final arbiter for the difficult choices. I believe it was at this time 1998–2000 two developments of major importance occurred: Firstly, Tony Blair opened the coffers of the Treasury and we were showered with money that had to be spent in the year – no proper planning – no co-ordination – and, if you don't know how to spend it, we were told, we will ask the private organisations to help. And secondly, the Private Finance Initiative was born, which saw a transformation of hospital buildings, new health centres and a corporate NHS philosophy of using the private sector to outsource laundry, parking, maintenance and IT services; as yet, no clinical services began. I think it was at this point that the patient was turned into a customer and consumer.

2006–2010 – It's too Difficult! Let the Patient Decide!

Nowhere has the change in social and cultural values been more felt than in Healthcare with the rise of the consumer movement and its effect on the power relationship between doctor and patient.

That knowledge is power is an axiom more true in medicine than almost any other aspect of our lives. Whilst the balance of knowledge is heavily weighted against the patient, it is very difficult for individuals to feel secure enough to challenge the professional or indeed that he has a right to know.

The rise of the consumer, user, customer and client in medicine has mirrored the gradual loss of deference towards authority whether expressed towards individuals or towards the traditional state apparatus of the Church, Parliament, Royal Family, legal profession and medicine. In medicine, the breaking down of the traditional roles has meant that agony aunts, professional journalists, social activist self-help groups, consumer organisations, managers and pharmaceutical companies have been able to provide information directly to the patient in a way that challenges the knowledge monopoly that the medical professional once held.

The Patient Charter, practice information booklets, participation groups, complaints procedures are all now part of modern health care. But it is not as simple as it looks. Firstly, the consumer speaks with many different tongues and any one individual consumer may speak differently at different times.

Both Labour and Conservative governments and the Coalition have been enthusiastic at promoting the patient/client/consumer/user voice, but have avoided the most difficult debates that we as a society need to have. What is the difference between a "want" and a "need" in a consumer led NHS? Most importantly, how long can we avoid talking about the elephant in the room – the "R" word – rationing? I will return to this omission later in my talk but we have some way to go yet. We are now entering our current phase of NHS development, where starting under the last Labour administration and continuing under the

Coalition we are inviting the private companies to bid for NHS contracts hoping they will solve the problems we face.

2010 – "We Give Up" – Call in the Private Companies

The NHS Bill, now Act of 2012, has used the strap line "extending patient choice". Essentially, it would seem we are now back in the mid-90s when practice-based commissioning was starting and the newly formed Clinical Commissioning Groups will take over from the Primary Care Trusts in commissioning services for the patient. What was not in the Bill and thus was never scrutinised by Parliament, or indeed the majority of the organisations that had major reservations of the Bill, were the implementation guidelines that are the substance of the next three presentations.

I will finish with two quotations:

Neo-Liberal

If we are to be prosperous we need more millionaires and more bankrupts.

(Keith Joseph)

Collectivist

A free health service is a triumphant example of the superiority of collective action and public initiative to a segment of society where commercial principles are seen at their worst.

(Aneurin Bevan)[29]

Notes

1 M. Balint (2000. First published 1957). *The Doctor, His Patient, and His Illness.* London. Churchill Livingstone.
2 RCGP (1972). The Future General Practitioner – Learning and Teaching. *The Journal of the Royal College of General Practitioners* 22(122). pp. 629–630.
3 The Department of Health & Social Security (1980). *Inequalities in Health: Report of a Research Working Group.* Black et al. Available at: www.sochealth. co.uk/national-health-service/public-health-and-wellbeing/poverty-and-inequality/ the-black-report-1980/. Last accessed: August 2022.
4 B. A. Tanner (Ed.) (1977). *Language and Communication in General Practice.* London. Hodder & Stoughton.
5 P. Pietroni (1981). Community Office Experience for Family Medicine Residents. *Journal of Medical Education* 56(1). pp. 8–15. Available at: https://journals.lww. com/academicmedicine/toc/1981/01000. Last accessed: August 2022.
6 Balint (2000. First published 1957). *Op. Cit.*
7 P. Pietroni (1989). The Doctor, His Patient, and His Illness: Michael Balint. *The British Journal of Psychiatry* 155(1). pp. 134–138.

112 Work, Professional Positions

8 P. Pietroni (1981). Community Office Experience for Family Medicine Residents. *Journal of Medical Education* 56(1). pp. 43–49.

9 P. Pietroni (1986). *Holistic Living: A Guide to Self-Care.* London. J. M. Dent.

10 P. Pietroni (1990). *The Greening of Medicine.* London. Gollancz.

11 C. Pietroni & P. Pietroni (1996). *Innovation in Community Care and Primary Health: The Marylebone Experiment.* Edinburgh. Livingstone.

12 P. Pietroni (2022). *The Poetry of Compassion Box Set.* Albuquerque. Fresco Books.

13 Gayle Lecture. *From Professional Autonomy to Practitioner Accountability.* Available at: https://ebrary.net/172376/education/care_concern_compassion_higher_education

14 D. Schon (1970). *Change and Industrial Society.* The Reith Lectures. Available at: www.bbc.co.uk/radio4/features/the-reith-lectures/transcripts/1970/. Last accessed: June 2022.

15 S. Harrison & C. Pollitt (1994). *Controlling Health Professionals: The Future of Work and Organization in the NHS.* Buckingham. Open University Press.

16 D. Schon (1987). The Crisis of Professional Knowledge and the Pursuit of an Epistemology of Practice. Delivered at Harvard Business School 75th Anniversary Colloquium on Teaching by the Case Method. Open University Press 52. Reprinted in *Journal of Interprofessional Care* 6(1). pp. 49–63 (1992).

17 Schon (1987). *Ibid.*

18 Schon (1987). *Ibid.*

19 G. Vickers (1984). *The Vickers Papers.* Cheltenham. Harper Collins. p. 152.

20 H. McCabe (2003). *God, Christ and us.* London: Continuum.

21 G. Vickers (Ed.) (2001. First published 1968). *Value Systems and Social Process.* Abington. Routledge.

22 S. Gyimah (2018). *Delivering Value for Money in the Age of the Student.* Speech at the 2018 Higher Education Policy Institute (UK) Annual Conference – From Funding to Fining: Universities in the new age of regulation. London. 7 June. Available at: www.gov.uk/government/speeches/delivering-value-for-money-in-the-age-of-the-student. Last accessed: July 2022.

23 International Conference on Health Promoting Universities and Colleges (2015). *Okanagan Charter: An International Charter for Health Promoting Universities and Colleges.* Available at: https://open.library.ubc.ca/cIRcle/collections/53926/items/1.0132754. Last accessed: May 2023.

24 D. Watson, R. Hollister, S. Stroud, & E. Babcock (2011). *The Engaged University: International Perspectives on Civic Engagement.* London: Routledge.

25 M. Thomas (2018). *Heroic Leadership is a Campus Villain.* Available at www.timeshighereducation.com/opinion/heroic-leadership-campus-villain. Last accessed June 2022.

26 D. M. Callejo Perez & J. Ode (Eds.) (2013). *The Stewardship of Higher Education: Re-imagining the Role of Education and Wellness on Community Impact.* Rotterdam. Sense Publishers.

27 M. Dooris, A. Farrier, & S. Powell (2018). *Healthy Universities: Whole University Leadership for Health, Wellbeing and Sustainability.* Available at: www.uclan.ac.uk/research/activity/healthy-universities-wellbeing-sustainability. Last accessed: June 2022.

28 P. Pietroni (2012). *Launching Conference of The Centre for Psychological Therapies in Primary Care. Why Are We Here?* University of Chester. Available at: https://www.chester.ac.uk/sites/files/chester/Learning%20From%20Each%20Other%20brochure%20%282%29.pdf. Last accessed: May 2023.

29 A. Bevan (1978. First published 1952). *In Place of Fear.* London. Quartet.

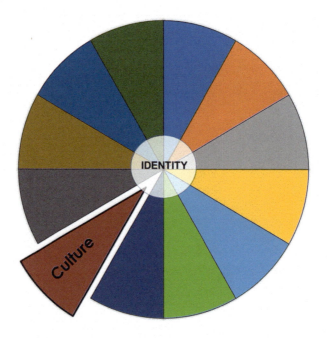

Figure 8.0

8 Culture, Culture Wars

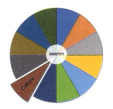

Figure 8.0

Introduction

Firstly, it is not an exaggeration to begin this chapter by acknowledging that the term *culture* can, and does, impact one's identity in a comprehensive and detailed way. The terms *culture studies; culture shock; culture wars; culture and society; culture and custom; multiculturalism; counter-culture* suggest the meaning attributed to the word *culture* is both fluid and contested.

Here are some of the definitions that have been constructed by academics over the years.

Richard Velkley:

> originally meant the cultivation of the soul or mind, acquires most of its later modern meanings in the writings of the 18th-century German thinkers, who on various levels developing Rousseau's criticism of modern liberalism and Enlightenment. Thus a contrast between "culture" and "civilization" is usually implied in these authors, even when not expressed as such.
>
> Refers to all the ways in which human beings overcome their original barbarism, and through artifice, become fully human.[1]

In the words of anthropologist E B Tylor, it is,

> that complex whole which includes knowledge, belief, art, law, morals, custom, and any other capabilities and habits acquired by man as a member of society.[2]

Alternatively, in a contemporary variant,

> Culture is defined as a social domain that emphasizes the practices, discourses, and material expressions, which, over time, express the continuities and discontinuities of social meaning of a life held in common.[3]

DOI: 10.4324/9781003401414-9

116   *Culture, Culture Wars*

I will limit myself to one more definition, if only to illustrate how the word culture provides for much disagreement. In 1986, philosopher Edward S Casey wrote,

> The very word culture meant 'place tilled' in Middle English, and the same word goes back to Latin colere, 'to inhabit, care for, till, worship' and cultus, 'A cult, especially a religious one. 'To be cultural, to have a culture, is to inhabit a place sufficiently intensely to cultivate it – to be responsible for it, to respond to it, to attend to it caringly.[4]

It is no wonder that we now find the words, culture shock; culture wars; culture studies and cultural elite emerge in our current discourse.

In section one (Biography), I will limit myself to describe how my own identity has evolved "culturally" through my likes and dislikes to some of the following "cultural pursuits": clothes; foods; sports; literature; art; music; film; theatre; alcohol; poetry; books; radio; games.

In section two, I will return to the extensive literature this word, culture, has produced, and focus on some of the recent concerns e.g. culture shock, multiculturalism and culture wars.

In section three, I will attempt to place my own current understanding of the term culture and how it has influenced my developing identity over my life time.

Section 1: Biography – My Cultural Pursuits

Explanatory Framework

In the table that follows, I have used a mixture of UK and US terminology to group the population (still predominantly White) of the Western world. The current debates and concerns regarding cultural wars, cultural crossroads and culture shock I will return to in section two.

	1	2	3	4
Population Designation	Masses	Hopeful	Elite	Powerful
Class Designation	Working Class	Middle Class	Upper Class	Super Class

Figure 8.1 Population and Class Designation

Using this formulation, I list my cultural pursuits and attempt to place them in one of the four columns they will mostly be identified with.

Culture, Culture Wars 117

Table of Cultural Pursuits

Area	Details	Identification
FOOD	French: Cheese, Ratatouille Greek: Moussaka, Yoghurt English: Roast Pork, Fish & Chips Italian: Alfredo Fettuccini, Pizza Spanish: Paella	3
ALCOHOL	Wine: Bordeaux Whiskey: Glen Livet Beer, Larger, Ricard, Pernod, Mojito, Margarita	3
CLOTHES	Three-piece suit, tie, cufflinks, flat cap, leather shoes	3
SPORT	Cricket: England Rugby: Wales Football: Arsenal	2/3
GAMES	Bridge, Chess, Solitaire, Backgammon	3
RADIO	BBC, Letter from America (Alistair Cooke), Something Understood (Mark Tully), In our Time (Melvin Bragg), News – BBC World Service	3
MUSIC	Opera: Verdi, Puccini Classical: Mahler, Beethoven, Mozart, Brahms Country & Western: Johnny Cash, Loretta Lynn Popular: The Beatles French: Charles Trenet, Edith Piaf	3
LITERATURE	History: Empires, World Affairs Biographies: Patrick Seymour VS Naipaul, Naomi Klein, E.M. Forster, Edward Said Post Modern	3
ART	Classic, Modern, Art Deco Picasso, Dali, Rembrandt	3
SCULPTURE	Modigliani	3
FILM	Westerns, French Casablanca, Gone with the Wind, The Red Balloon	3
NEWSPAPERS	Guardian (UK), New York Times (USA)	3
THEATRE	Shakespeare, Oscar Wild, Anton Chekhov, Arthur Miller, Alan Ayckbourn, Harold Pinter	3
POETRY	T S Elliot, Thomas Hardy, Edward Thomas, Rudyard Kipling, Rupert Brooke, Mary Angelou, Rumi, Pablo Neruda, Mary Oliver Samuel Taylor Coleridge, Sylvia Plath, Elizabeth Browning, Emily Dickenson	3

Figure 8.2 Table of Cultural Pursuits

118   *Culture, Culture Wars*

I think from this list it is clear that I at least consider myself one of the educated elite!

I should add a list of my dislikes which are as important as my likes:

Cultural Dislikes

CLOTHES T-shirts, baseball hats, sneakers, modern fashion – as it applies to both men and woman
TV   Most of what is on popular TV
FOOD   Fast food, red meat, take-aways
MUSIC   Most modern popular music
FILMS   Sci-fi
ALCOHOL Cheap wine

It is clear from this list that I am a cultural snob and stuck in my belief of myself as part of the elite.

Section 2 – Academic Studies of Culture

As indicated in the introduction, the concept of culture is so enormous that it has become a separate area of study:

Cultural Studies

There cannot be very many other words that have added additional epithets before and after the word culture: multicultural; acculturation; popular culture; cultural norms; primitive culture; cultural wars; culture shock, cultural crossroads; cultural lens; cultural practices; cultural elite; counter-culture. Indeed, it needs to be admitted that cultural studies have become a CULT in their own right.

I will limit myself to the early academic focus on the word culture and the very most recent emergence of the word, as used in the term, culture wars. I have quoted in the introduction some of the earlier definitions of culture, and it is important to remember its agricultural origins, "to cultivate". As Cicero writes, "*it is the cultivation of the mind/soul*".[5] "Cultura Animi" – he was focussing on.

Culture was very much part of the Renaissance/Enlightenment years. The Romantics, both German (Kant, Bastian) as well as the English Romantics (Hobbs, Coleridge) and the French Romantics all regarded the acquisition of wisdom followed the acquisition of cultural pursuits. Thus studying arts, literature, music, poetry etc. became the rungs of the ladder that allowed you to become cultured.

The "ologies" then took over and each one of them declared their "cultural lens" was the one through which culture could be both understood and acquired:

psychology; anthropology; sociology. And need we include the non-ologies: philosophy; education; politics; genetics, and more recently and importantly, postmodernism.

The Emergence of "Culture Wars"

The mid-sixties saw the emergence of post-modernism and the use of aspects of Marxism to interrogate the concept of culture. Most influential were a group of UK sociologists who borrowed from the Frankfurt school of Marxism to develop and construct the "cultural lens" of "Postmodernism". The names associated with this movement include: Stuart Hall; Raymond Williams; Paul Gilroy; E P Thomas and Richard Hoggart. Many drew on the psychoanalytic theory of Louis Althusser and the feminist, Julia Kristeva.

I hesitate to try and summarise these learned scholars, except to say their focus was on the meaning that underpinned a particular cultural norm e.g. why fish and chips or Indian curry are considered to be a cultural "like" for the working class, and oysters and foie gras is the food served to the elite. This fact brings to light that popular culture and "high culture" are related to money, wealth and class. Why should opera (very expensive) be considered "high culture" and popular concerts (hip-hop, country and western) be considered "low culture"? This argument can be expanded i.e. literature; art; sport; religion and healthcare.

With the emergence of Donald Trump, the whole issue of culture wars became politicised to include many of the following cultural labels:

1. Sexual orientation and gender issues
2. Birth control and abortion laws
3. Euthanasia and freedom to choose
4. Vaccination and wearing masks
5. Gun rights
6. Brexit and replacing the metric system in the UK
7. Climate change and fossil fuels
8. Removal of confederal statues
9. Admission of colonial mass-extinction
10. Control of immigration
11. Conservative values vs progressive politics

Evidence of the emergence of cultural wars can be seen in the emergence of:

1. Black Lives Matter movement
2. The Me Too movement
3. Trump MAGA (Make America Great Again), which is a cover for MAWA (Make America White Again)
4. The attack and attempt to alter the voting rights

120   *Culture, Culture Wars*

Books aplenty and newspaper headlines affirm that we are now in the state of culture shock, a culture crossroads and culture wars.

Much of this development has occurred on the digital platforms – the radio and television. News programmes, each adopt a position in the culture wars. As a result, the protection of culture has also become politicised. The United Nations established UNESCO and passed Article 27 of the Human Rights Act which provided protection for the cultural heritage of all societies to be recognised as a legal right. We, however, continue to witness the destruction of cultural buildings (churches; mosques; Buddhist temples; military statues) as an essential target in times of war.

Section 3

I have laid open my own cultural identity in the first section of this chapter and have to acknowledge the choices I have made are inevitably accompanied by unconscious bias.

How many likes and dislikes I listed have allowed me to consider myself part of the privileged/monied elite? How much of these "identificats" require a level of wealth shared only by 10% of the population? How much are they the consequence of a privileged education? How much do they require access to activities (film; books; concerts; theatre; art galleries) that are available to only those with wealth? More importantly, how does this (my) section of society maintain its cultural pastimes and privilege through charitable donations (which are tax exempt) and bribery? How many parents donate to the Harvards and Oxfords of the university world to ensure their children attend these educational establishments? The parents can be assured that these centres of learning will encourage, foster, teach these high cultural pursuits – philosophy; classical music; opera; the canon of Western literature – Shakespeare; Milton; Plato; Cicero etc. And how much do these charitable donations (again, tax exempt) allow for subsidising high art in galleries (MOMA), annual festivals of films (Cannes), opera (Metropolitan, New York) and the restoration of ancient monuments (Delphi – Temple of Apollo)?

Since the beginning of the 1980s, the culture wars have become increasingly politicised and received a major boost during the 2016 Presidential Election, when Donald Trump was successful in winning the Republican candidacy, and went on to defeat Hilary Clinton. Another feature of the culture wars emerged following Tump's defeat in 2020 – voting fraud and "Stop the Steal" became a far more serious development and resulted in the January 6th uprising attack of the Congress building. During the current Covid epidemic, the wearing of masks and vaccination were added to the list that has divided the United States in an unprecedented separation which continues to paralyse effective government by the current President, Joe Biden. For the first time in modern history, this serious and dangerous split has already involved the Supreme Court in the prohibition of all abortion within the State of Texas, to include those women who are pregnant as a result of rape.

Time magazine published a paper *How America's elites lost their grip*.[6] I have identified myself as part of the elite and no, I have not "lost my grip", but I do not see any likelihood of a restoration of these culture wars, and fear for the peaceful future and collapse of "The American Dream".

Notes

1 R. L. Velkley (2002). The Tension in the Beautiful: On Culture and Civilization in Rousseau and German Philosophy. In *Being After Rousseau: Philosophy and Culture in Question*. pp. 11–30. Chicago. The University of Chicago Press.
2 E. B. Tylor (1920. Originally published 1871). *Primitive Culture: Researches into the Development of Mythology, Philosophy, Religion, Language, Art, and Custom*. London. John Murray. Available at: https://archive.org/details/in.ernet.dli.2015.42334/page/n11/mode/2up. Last accessed: June 2022.
3 Tylor (1920. Originally published 1871). *Ibid*.
4 K. Sorrells (Ed.) (2013). *Intercultural Communication: Globalization and Social Justice*. Los Angeles. Sage.
5 M. T. Cicero & W. Melmoth (Trans.) (1889). *Old Age and Friendship*. Cassell's National Library no. 195.
6 A. Giridharadas (2019). How America's Elites Lost Their Grip. *Time* 21 November.

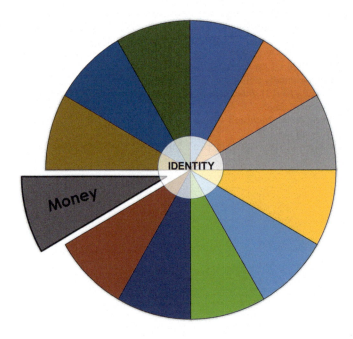

Figure 9.0

9 Money, Wealth, Status

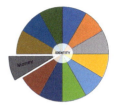

Figure 9.0

Introduction

In this chapter I describe and explore how my family of origin and my own family have related to the three words – money, wealth and status. I expand on the concept of economics in Chapter 11, when I address how political and economic theory have impacted on our "chosen" identity.

Section 1: Biography

My father was a successful doctor, and my mother never worked. Neither of them inherited any money from their parents, and so our own "wealth" was dependant on my father's income. It would be fair to say we were never considered to be "rich", even though we always had live-in maids, and my father employed a secretary and chauffeur. This suggests that although we may not have been rich, we were certainly "wealthy" in comparison to the 90% of the rest of the population of Cyprus.

My parents had "wealthy" friends with much larger homes than we had, often with an outside swimming pool and a car that only wealthy folk could afford. Notwithstanding our relative poverty, my father gave us a status in the community that reflected the respect given to him as a result of his professional standing. We were all sent to the English School (term fees £9.00 a year) and all four sons went onto be accepted at Guy's Hospital Medical School in London (fees paid for the two eldest sons by the Colonial Government).

Our father kept separate red note books for each of us and every month we would meet with him and he recorded how much of our previous pocket money we had spent and how much he gave each one of us a month. The amounts were linked to our age, and on those occasions if you hadn't spent all your pocket money of the previous month you would receive a bonus in addition to your monthly allowance. We each of us had the traditional money box (*tirelire*, in French) that some of us kept our money in. I spent most, if not all, my monthly allowance on buying English boys magazines, and got to know the likes of

DOI: 10.4324/9781003401414-10

124 *Money, Wealth, Status*

Captain Marvel and Billy Bunter at an early age. Other spending included marbles, which was a very popular pastime. As I grew older I would buy stamps and the Stanley Gibbon magazine. Another of my father's "schemes" was to promise to give us £100 if we had not smoked by the time we were 21. None of us did smoke, and I only started smoking a pipe in my mid-thirties (my father smoked a pipe!). Our mother had jewellery and fur coats, all appropriate for the time and culture of the time. We did not have an overseas holiday until I was sixteen, when we went on a cruise to Greece. My experience of both a rich and wealthy family was when we visited my Armenian Uncle's home (he married my father's sister). Now, there was wealth! Persian/Turkish carpets, maids dressed in uniform, billiard tables, table-tennis room, and beautiful garden with fountains and maze. The best item I remember was the car: a green Cadillac. My uncle, a wealthy business man, I do believe, shared some of his wealth with the rest of the family, and I believe he "owned" the house we lived in, throughout my early years.

In 1960 I went to London to start my medical education. I joined my brothers who were already at medical school, and for a year we all shared "student digs" close to Guy's Hospital. At this stage we were all supported by a grant from the Colonial Cyprus Government. In 1961 my father decided to leave Cyprus and arrived in London, where he eventually settled in West London (Shepherds Bush). He was now having to support us all as we no longer had the Cyprus Government financial support. This meant he could no longer support our living away from home, and all three sons moved back to the family home. My eldest brother had qualified as a doctor, got married and obtained a job as a junior doctor.

In order to help the family finances I, for the rest of my medical student years, had a series of paid jobs in the evening and during the holiday periods. I think I was paid £3.00 an hour, and this allowed me some independence. Half way through my medical student yeas, I joined the Royal Army Medical Cadet scheme, and was then fully supported by the army (£700 a year) for the next three years as a medical student. Once qualified as a doctor I had the rank of Captain in the army and was able to support my wife and our three children. We bought our first house in Folkestone in 1968 for £9,000. I cannot remember being concerned about our finances, as my wife also worked part-time as a locum doctor, and for the next three-four years we lived comfortably on my army pay.

I left the army in 1970, joined my father in his medical practice and for the next ten years or so lived on my general practice salary. Aged 30 in 1972 we bought a beautiful three storey Georgian house in Ealing (West London), and I recall how proud and contented I was celebrating my wife's 30th birthday in our magnificent new home. Not rich, but certainly wealthy. We also had bought, together with my brother, a lovely 18th Century cottage on the Norfolk Broads, where we spent many happy weekends and summer holidays.

Divorce in 1975 brought everything to a halt, and for a while I lived on my own in a rented apartment. I met my second wife soon after, and we left for the United States when I obtained my first academic appointment at the University of Cincinnati. My career continued to develop, and I was soon a full professor and eventually a postgraduate Dean at London University. In addition to my academic salary I also had developed a busy private psychoanalytic practice, and together with the many research grants I obtained, was increasingly comfortable with my annual salary.

I married my second wife in 1977, and we bought our London home in Primrose Hill for a six figure sum. We sold it eventually for eight times the price we paid, so our finances were more than enough to support our lifestyle. In 1985 we bought an empty and charming small farmhouse in the Dordogne (France) and eventually converted it into a most wonderful weekend and holiday home. My wife rediscovered her love of horse riding and we developed our French home to include stables; riding ring; swimming pool; tennis court and beautiful garden – and yes, now it felt as if we were rich (had money), wealthy and had "status". A further development allowed me to experience some of the more disreputable areas of the financial world. I received an invitation to become a non-executive director of a new company to be established by one of our well-known city banks. The company was established to provide our National Health Service with up-to-date primary care general practices and hospital new builds. I was to provide and oversee the design and layout of these new and "state of the art" medical facilities. The board of this company had six directors, all financial experts in the City of London. I was interviewed by the chairman and invited to invest my own money, and thus take part in the profits that would accrue. I declined, but joined the board (paid an annual four-figure sum). We met in the boardroom of the bank underpinning the project and within a year had "floated" the company on the stock exchange. We bought up old and run-down general practices and designed and built new facilities and then "rented" them out to the NHS. This all seemed acceptable to me until at one board meeting I, ignorant as I was on financial matters, learnt why we were so successful with making a huge profit so early in our existence. Here is how I understood it worked: we borrowed large sums of money from the City on 26th of the month – four days before we had to pay our bills. During those four days we used the money to reinvest in the other profitable companies. Our investment director was able to ensure we made far more profit each month which had nothing to do with the expressed function of our company (new builds rented out to the NHS). In fact, none of the directors were particularly interested in our supposed primary function. After the third year, when we had "floated" on the stock exchange, I was again invited to buy some of the shares in our company, and as a director, I was able to buy them at a fixed low price and would make a profit of over 20%. We had by then sold our property in Primrose Hill, and I invested £500,000. Disaster was to follow the following year when I decided to sell my shares. Unknowingly, I chose to do

126 *Money, Wealth, Status*

this at the time when we had not declared our dividend, and I thus was reported to the City authorities for "insider dealing". I had my wrists smartly slapped and resigned from the board having learned the lesson that I was not suited to high finance.

Soon after this so sorry episode I took early retirement from the NHS, and am quite happy with my pension pot, together with my earnings from my psycho-analytic practice.

Section 2: The Literature on Money, Wealth and Status

There are whole libraries available on those subjects and I do not pretend to cover them here in any great detail. I have tried to summarise my own preju-diced, no doubt, understanding of how I currently "identify" their meaning.

Money

First, a poem:

LOVE-MONEY AND US

A lady once wrote
"How do I love you?
Let me count the way."

That was some time ago
And she never mentioned money.
Times have changed.
We are all captured by
Un-regulated market forces.
All is now commodified,
Categorised and sold.
All our transactions priced.

Does love now have a price?
Yes, of course it has,
But its value cannot be
Counted in Dollars/Pounds or Yen.

Your love appeared at the Lion Hotel,
Your eyes sparkled like diamonds,
Your voice was gentle and soft.
We soon found ourselves naked together,
And I delved into the treasures of your body.

But you are rich as well,
Richer than all the money you have,
Richer still because you share your riches.
Those who you give to
Only receive your money
And remain far poorer than I do,
For you give me what
Money can never buy.

No money could buy what you give,
And no money is needed to continue.
Our love is priceless and not for sale.
No shareholders need apply.
It will remain with us,
To enjoy and spend as we wish.

Anon[1]

Niall Ferguson's book, *The Ascent of Money*[2] charts the emergence of money – finance, monetary policy, the stock market and yes, the descent of money. I will quote some of the central passages from his book:

Money, it is conventional to argue, is a medium of exchange, which has the advantage of eliminating inefficiencies of barter; a unit of account, which facilitates valuation and calculation; and a store of value, which allows economic transactions to be conducted over long periods as well as geographical distances. To perform all these functions optimally, money has to be available, affordable, durable, fungible, portable and reliable. Because they fulfil most of these criteria, metals such as gold, silver and bronze were for millennia regarded as the ideal monetary raw material. The earliest known coins date back as long ago as 600 BC and were found by archaeologists in the Temple of Artemis at Ephesus (near Izmir in modern-day Turkey). These ovular Lydian coins, which were made of the gold-silver alloy known as electrum and bore the image of a lion's head were the forerunners of the Athenian tetradrachm, a standardized silver coin with the head of the goddess Athena on one side and an owl (associated with her for its supposed wisdom) on the obverse. By Roman times, coins were produced in their different metals: the aureus (gold), the denarius (silver) and the sestertius (bronze), ranked in that order according to the relative scarcity of the metals in question, but all bearing the head of the reigning emperor on one side, and the legendary figures of Romulus and Remus on the other. Coins were not unique to the ancient Mediterranean, but they clearly arose there first. It was not until 221 BC that a standardized bronze coin was introduced to China by the 'first Emperor', Qin Shihuangdi. In each case, coins made of precious metal were associated with

128 *Money, Wealth, Status*

powerful sovereigns who monopolized the minting of money so as to exploit it as a source of revenue.[3]

The invention of money ensured that the "human relational" quality of bartering was replaced by the anonymous, transactional quality and the invention of the market stock exchange, bonds, derivatives, bear/bull markets, leverage, securities banks clearing houses, The Federal Reserve boom and bust liquidity crises and the bit coin. And of course, the Lehman Brothers bankruptcy and the 2008 crash, which nearly caused governments to fall, unemployment to rise and income inequality between the rich and the poor to become morally unacceptable.

Those arguing for what has been labelled as "creative destruction" will point out:

> There is no longer much doubt that free commerce has a better economic or humanitarian record than command-and-control government. The examples just keep rolling in. Take the history of Sweden, for instance. Contrary to conventional wisdom, Sweden did not become wealthy as a result of having a big government imposing social democracy. When it liberalized a feudal economy and strongly embraced Smithian free trade and free markets in the 1860s, the result was rapid growth and the spawning of the great enterprises over the next fifty years, new products. When it expanded government hugely in the 1970s, the result was currency devaluation, stagnation and slow growth, culminating in a full-blown economic crisis in 1992 and a rapid fall in the country's relative standing in the world's economic league table. When it cut taxes, privatised education and liberalised private healthcare in the 2000s, it rediscovered growth.
>
> Prosperity emerged despite, not because of, human policy. It developed inexorably out of the inter action of people by a form of selective progress very similar to evolution. Above all, it was a decentralized phenomenon, achieved by millions of individual decisions, mostly in spite of the actions of rulers.[4]

Commentary on the aforementioned position is explored in depth in Philip Roscoe's book, *I spend therefore I am: the true cost of economics*, and he states, *"Selfish competition is the essence of economic theory"*.[5]

Wealth

1) A quote, 2) a statistic, and 3) A poem, and my personal view:

> 1) There is enough for everyone's need, but not enough for everyone's greed.[6]
> 2) 1% of adults hold 46% of world wealth[7]
> 3) **The Highwayman**

As a man lost in thoughts walked past
highwayman roared
awakened by the solid shout
the poor man replied
there is not one penny in the pocket
nor a grain in the house
my family waiting for me for some grain
for cooking the dinner

Is it so, let me see
he was checked and allowed to go home
he then made a humble request
can you please lend me a penny
smiling highwayman replied

taking the risk has a cost
it has to be offset by earning profit
charity is free lunch
there is no free lunch in business

go home you'll get used to hunger
or take my offer
get trained in this art
I am expanding my venture

If you are interested, sign, here
and take this penny

Ramachandran Rajasekharan[8]

That is all you need to know!

My own personal view:

It has taken many decades for us to introduce a minimum wage for the majority of the workforce at the bottom of the ladder.

Until we introduce a maximum wage for those 1% at the top of the ladder, we will continue to push humanity over the precipice to destruction.

If we don't alter our economic system the perils of climate change will force us so to do.

We have two choices left to us:

1. Man the pumps or
2. Launch the life boats

P.S. Suggested reading – any of the hundreds of books written on this subject.

Money, Wealth, Status

Status

Status is a fluid term that can be inherited, as in the offspring of a royal family, or linked to professional achievement e.g. judge or architect. It can be linked to sporting achievement or wealth, or linked to the class structure and nationality. A big fish in a small pond has status, but not when he/she is no longer in his/her small pond. Criminal behaviour or acts of corruption can destroy someone's status, from which they may never recover. Status can be linked to wealth, but this will not occur if the wealth is the result of criminal behaviour. Although, some famous criminals achieve status. Social status can differ from professional status, so that attributing status will differ in its construct e.g. a heavyweight boxer may achieve status but will be awarded a different set of attributes than a successful surgeon. Heroic behaviour in times of war, or danger, immediately confers status, which can be remembered for centuries and be used as an exemplar. Achieving status may propel someone from a lower social class to become an honorary member of a higher class, and in the UK it will allow him/her to become a member the House of Lords.

Section 3: Linking Biography with Academic Literature

It is undoubtedly true that I achieved success in all the three areas covered in this chapter. I earnt enough money to look after my family and my retirement. Although, neither rich nor wealthy by the standards often used to measure such description, we had enough money for all our needs and lived a comfortable and enjoyable life commensurate with our status. The status I achieved was the result of my professional achievements, my academic publications and books written. During the time I worked as Prince Charles' medical advisor I was often mentioned in newspapers, and the BBC did a half-hour programme of our work at the Marylebone Health Centre. It is essential that I also accept that success in all three domains were by no means the whole picture, and all too often I may have succumbed to using this "identity" to counteract other "identities" not so flattering as described in this chapter but outlined in many of the others.

Notes

1 Anon (2022). *Love-Money and Us.*
2 N. Ferguson (2008). *The Ascent of Money: A Financial History of the World.* London. Penguin.
3 Ferguson (2008). *Ibid.*
4 Ferguson (2008). *Ibid.*
5 P. Roscoe (2014). *I Spend, Therefore I Am: The True Cost of Economics.* London. Viking.
6 Anon (2022). *Op. Cit.*
7 Roscoe (2014). *Op. Cit.*
8 R. Rajasekharan (2020). *The Highwayman.* Available at: https://allpoetry.com/poem/15581841-The-highwayman-by-RamachandranRajasekhar. Last accessed: July 2022.

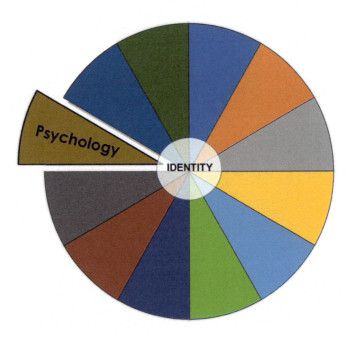

Figure 10.0

10 Psychology, Psychiatry, Psychoanalysis

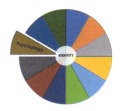

Figure 10.0

Section 1: Biography

This chapter is the most challenging for me to write. I have found Dr Pragya Agarwal's book, *Sway: Unravelling Unconscious Bias*[1] enormously helpful in understanding why. He addresses the issue of unconscious bias and

> Unravels the way we communicate and perceive the world, and how this affects the way we communicate and perceive the world.[2]

Agarwal explores the question, *"If we don't know when our biases are activated, are we really responsible for it?"*[3]

Later on in this chapter I attempt to describe my own journey as a psychoanalyst, which attempts to bring these unconscious biases into consciousness, or not as the case may be.

Firstly, let me start with a brief summary of what I am conscious of as a result of the psychological tests I have taken.

<u>Myers Briggs</u> (test available at: www.themyersbriggs.com/en-US/Company/News/Psychometric-Testing)

I will elaborate in greater detail in section 2, but over the years that I have taken this test, I have remained classified as "INFP".

I = introversion
N = intuition
F= Feeling
P = Perception

My extroversion and introversion scores are often interchangeable, but I score INFP more often than I score EFTP. There are 16 possible "types" using Myers Briggs Type Indicator (MBTI), and David Keirsey has used the word "temperaments" to describe all 16 types and has given each a label all positive (this must

DOI: 10.4324/9781003401414-11

Figure 10.1 Myers Briggs

be wrong). INFP carries the label "Healer" and ENFP is labelled "Champion". I return to this later.

IQ Score

More simple, more straightforward and more reliable, is the IQ scoring method; mine is 129. I must own up at this point to admit my own prejudice (unconscious bias?) against psychologists when they use numbers to determine personality disorders. There is an old Cypriot proverb,

> A fool throws a stone into the sea, and a thousand wise men cannot pull it out.

I have previously described my early childhood experience:

1. No breast-feeding by my mother
2. Night terrors and bedwetting until aged 11
3. Guilt and shame linked to masturbation
4. Development of competitive and aggressive behaviour – "kill, kill, kill!"

I will now outline how I remember those early and later experiences that helped to shape the "better side of my angels".

I hero worshiped my eldest brother, although he paid little attention to me. I bullied and ignored my youngest brother, and the consequences still remain. I did, however, form a close and emotionally attached relationship with my elder brother (two years older than me). We invented a private language between us,

Psychology, Psychiatry, Psychoanalysis 135

and would great each other with the question, "how are our little men doing?". My first kiss happened on my 14th birthday, and my first girlfriend when I was 16. I do not remember ever being consoled when frightened or troubled by either of my parents. I do remember falling off my bicycle aged 12 and hurting my knee, which was bleeding. My father was busy with his patients and my mother phoned my Uncle (my father's brother), who came over to our house immediately, and I still can recollect the tender and caring way he bandaged my knee (I wish he had been my father). These are all negative memories and experiences which suggest I was both needy and unhappy. However, it is also true that I responded by becoming competitive and aggressive, hiding my sense of vulnerability and neediness;

> Attachment behaviour . . . is a form of instinctive behaviour that develops in humans, as in other mammals, during infancy, and has as its aim or goal/proximity to a mother-figure. The function of attachment behaviour, it is suggested, is protection from predators. Whilst attachment behaviour is shown especially strongly during childhood when it is directed towards parent figures, it none the less continues to be active during adult life when it is usually directed towards some active and dominant figure, often a relative but sometimes an employer or some elder of the community. Attachment behaviour, the theory emphasises, is elicited when a person (child or adult) is stick or in trouble, and is elicited at high intensity when he is frightened or when the attachment-figure cannot be found. Because, in the light of this theory, attachment behaviour is regarded as a normal and healthy part of man's instinctive makeup, it is held to be most misleading to term it 'regressive' or childish when seen in an older child or adult. For this reason, too, the term 'dependency' is regarded as leading to a seriously mistaken perspective, for in everyday speech to describe someone as dependent cannot help carrying with it overtones of criticism. By contract, to describe someone as attached carries with it a positive evaluation.[4]

Where I did find safety was in my bed where I covered myself with the blankets and turned my face to the wall, hugging my pillow (so I would not see the "ogre" who had come to kill me). I, in effect, constructed as safe a cocoon as I could manage to create. For some 20–40 years, as an adult, I have built sheds for myself (sheds in the garden, sheds for my books, sheds for my tools, and sheds to eat and drink in).

My two parents decided that we should all call them by their first name, Michel and Jeanette. Thus we never called them Dad/Daddy or Mummy. I do believe this ensured we did not have a concept of Dad or Mum, and I suspect this had an important influence on our psychological relationship with them. I called my grandfather, Papou (Greek) and my grandmother, Ya Ya (Greek); my aunts I called, Tante (French) and my uncles, Oncle (French). I am not aware whether this choice of names has been studied anywhere, but I know I had a

136 *Psychology, Psychiatry, Psychoanalysis*

closer emotional link with my grandparents, uncles and aunts. My first experience, and subsequently my first "love" was the daughter of a squadron leader whom I knew as Ricky. I was 16 and she was 14. We went "out" together and I fell head-over-heels in love with her. This lasted only 18 months or so, when, to use the parlance of the era, she "jilted" me for a much older man. I was devastated and felt abandoned, and was not able to disclose this episode to anyone. We met again when I had left my wife and rekindled our love. This again broke down after 18 months, but we send each other birthday letters and presents. There is an excellent little book on first loves[5] which I found very helpful on both understanding and disengaging from my first "attachment" feminine/mother figure. I very soon "fell in love" with my fellow medical student in the second year of my medical school year, and married when we were both approaching our 2nd year. We had three children and separated 13 years later.

We had few, if any, "psychological" courses at medical school and the psychiatry training we received was focussed solely on the physical aspect of mental health. The psychiatrist who taught us focussed on the pharmaceutical treatment of mental health disorders: depression; anxiety; schizophrenia; dementia. As mentioned earlier, I took part in the use of ECT (electroconvulsive therapy), and on one occasion this involved a young (22 years old) homosexual "patient".

My psychological education started once I had become a general practitioner, and I was heavily influenced by the work of Michael Balint – a Hungarian psychoanalyst whose book, *The Doctor, his patient and the illness*[6] became my bible, and still is.

The best known approach for teaching psychological diagnosis has been the Balint group (https://balint.co.uk/about/the-balint-method/). Other methods have involved the use of role-play, simulated patient interviews and video-tape playback. Heron (https://challengingcoaching.co.uk/herons-six-categories-of-intervention/) had described his approach to developing a 'peer learning group' using some of the 'growth exercises' that arose out of the Human Potential Movement.

Initially, seminars on teaching skills relied heavily on the methodology developed by educationalists. Many general practitioners learnt about 'defining education objectives', 'giving feed-back' and preparing 'assessment questionnaires'; Marinker (1972)[7] described the outcome of the London Teacher's Workshop in which an attempt was made to look at the problems of trainer/trainee relationship in some depth.

Subsequent courses included Freeling and Barry's Nuffield Course for Trainers[8] and Byrne and Long's work at Manchester.[9] The tasks of these courses can be summarised by one of the following categories:

1. To increase the doctor's sensitivity to the over-all needs of the patient/trainee.
2. To increase the doctor's sensitivity to the important part his personality plays in managing the problems of the patient/trainee.
3. To increase the doctor's skill in being a member of and leading a small group.

Psychology, Psychiatry, Psychoanalysis 137

Balint's "interpenetrating mix-up" is one of his most delightful phrases and captures the true nature of the best of general practice. Balint refers to two kinds of medicine, one where illness is seen as an accident arising from causes outside the patient and where the basis of rational therapy arises out of a theory about the causation of illness and the control of the presumed cause. The second is where illness is seen as a lack of integration between the individual and the environment and a meaningful phase in the patient's life. Here, meaning is used to imply purpose as opposed to cause.

I later became a senior trainer myself, and on Balint's anniversary of the publication of his book I was asked and wrote a summary of his work and the influence he had had on general practitioners. It was indeed his influence that propelled me to undertake a psychoanalytic training myself. My two episodes of teaching in the United States brought me into contact with the encounter group, humanistic psychology and Gestalt models of understanding the nature of the work of a family doctor. It was an incidental and unplanned meeting with a yellow cab driver in New York that lit the flame for the next period of my psychological development.

Sitting in the back of a yellow cab in New York, going to the airport, I got into conversation with the driver whose name, as stated on the dashboard, was John Smith. He was about my age, black hair and beard. I asked him why he was driving his cab, this is, as I remember, his reply:

> I was always getting into trouble at my school and work, my family came from Jordan. Although I was born in New York, I decided one day I would go to Jordan and visit my ancestral home. I discovered my family were part of a nomadic Hashemite tribe and my original name was Gideon Ben Barrak. My tribe was nomadic and travelled over the Middle East on camels and never settled anywhere for any length of time. I joined, and loved the life of a nomad for three years, and realised this way of life was in my genes and my blood. I returned to New York and bought a campervan and travelled around the States, never staying anywhere for too long. When I need to earn some money I come back to New York and drive a cab for a month or so, then I go back to my campervan – which is what I am about to do after I take you to the airport.

Silenced by this story, I eventually said, "*I live in Chapel Hill (North Carolina). If you are ever in this area, drop in to see me*". And I gave him my address. Three weeks later he appeared at my door and stayed with me for three weeks. I realised immediately that his need for a campervan and my need for a shed were not that dissimilar, and my own nomadic tendencies were also part of my heritage. I returned to the UK and immediately applied for a Jungian psychoanalytic training, and have continued to build sheds wherever I live.

138 *Psychology, Psychiatry, Psychoanalysis*

YOGA AND EASTERN PHILOSOPHY
I have outlined my time at the Himalayan Institute and guru in Chapter 3.

Psychoanalytic Training

When I returned from the States I was appointed a senior lecturer at St Mary's Hospital in London and soon after met, and married, my second wife, who was finishing her training as a psychotherapist at the Tavistock Clinic. The Tavi, as it was called, was at the time the Mecca for all those who wished to train as a psychotherapist/psychoanalyst. I not only learnt from my new wife, but was introduced to the leaders and trainers of the psychoanalytic fraternity. It became clear to me that my status as a senior general practitioner was not viewed with the level of academic excellence that I had assumed it had. In my application to become a trainee I was asked the following question:

What influences have contributed to your decision to apply for training as an analytical psychologist?

I wrote:

Jung's writings and the practice of analytical psychology are the nearest to meeting my own current perceptions and Weltanschauung. I am particularly looking forward to a more detailed study of the Self as outlined by Jung and his followers. I am especially interested in the links Jung made with Eastern thought and literature.

I have been seeing patients in a therapeutic setting for some time and would value and benefit from individual supervision. The discipline of reporting my work to an experienced analyst is one that I have not had.

I have a number of professional colleagues who are analytical psychologists and find their friendship important. I find I share, by and large, their views and values.

I see my career developing in such a way as to encompass a physical, psychological and spiritual approach toward the care of my patients. The training in analytical psychology would help to underpin at least two of those aspects.

For the next five years I attended weekly seminars, saw my analyst three-five times a week, and in the last two years saw two training clients in analysis three-five times a week, followed by weekly supervision from my two supervisors.

I outline one session in my analysis that became a block to my development:

On one occasion lying on the couch I exploded with rage, fury and hate, and to my horror my analyst (an elderly, kind and sensitive lady) responded by developing chest pain and angina attack. I had to rapidly move into doctor mode and look after her. After she recovered we terminated the session and she went off

Psychology, Psychiatry, Psychoanalysis   139

to see her own doctor. I never again allowed myself to explode in my sessions, to my detriment.

It was a far better and thorough training than the one I had experienced at medical school, and for a while we would meet once a year after all graduating. I never regretted choosing a Jungian training, although this was viewed with major suspicion by the "elite" at the Tavistock Clinic.

My wife at the time had had a Freudian/Kleinian training and I do believe we each enriched our knowledge by the discussions and sharing that we were able to have. After qualifying as a Jungian analyst, I developed a busy practice where I saw clients at our home whilst still practising as a GP. I eventually became a trainer myself, and I would supervise trainee analysts.

Section 2: Academic Literature

It is with trepidation that I presume I can summarise the issues that psychology, psychiatry and psychoanalysis, but what follows is a helicopter ride over the terrain which, hopefully, can fill some of the gaps that are missing in my biographical section.

MODELS OF THE MIND

We take it for granted that our mind is in some way linked with our brain; if it resides anywhere, it must be somewhere in our head. In fact, this is a relatively recent notion, for the Egyptians believed that mind-spirit-soul resided not in the brain but in the bowels and heart. The Sumerians thought it resided in the liver and even the great philosopher Aristotle saw the heart as the seat of thought and feeling. Aristotle and Plato, his teacher, were the major Western philosophers whose opinions concerning the mind held sway right from 300 BC until the sixteenth and seventeenth centuries. Even now, the study of the mind is hampered by the descriptions outlined thousands of years ago by these two great men. Their observations were a great step forward, but because of their greatness few individuals had the courage to build on their descriptions. The relationship between Plato and Aristotle is beautifully expressed in Raphael's majestic fresco "The School of Athens". There we see Plato, with hand upraised pointing to the stars, whereas Aristotle, holding a copy of Plato's book *Timaeus*, is pointing to the earth. Although Plato is seen as a great rationalist, he did not believe in trusting the senses and arrived at his great description of the mind, knowledge and civilisation through a mixture of mystical contemplation and mathematics. Plato's *Republic* gives a description as to how he saw the perfect civilisation. The outline is based on an oligarchy (government by the few) and Plato's ideas are relatively hierarchical. Because he valued reason above all other attributes, it followed that it should reside in the topmost part of the body – the head. Plato felt knowledge was better acquired not from observation but through "vision of truth", and the parable of "the cave" is his clearest description of how man is entrapped and chained by his limited visions.

Figure 10.2 The School of Athens

Aristotle was far more of a realist than Plato and was himself a great biologist. It is ironic that he felt the heart to be the seat of life, the soul and the mind, and the brain function was the blood that carried the life-force through the body. However, although Aristotle's observations were inaccurate, they were balanced by his foundation of the system of deductive logic which still governs the principles of rational debate to this day. Both Plato and Aristotle were instrumental in seeing the mind's chief faculty as reason and logic, and the early Christian church incorporated some aspects of their philosophies. The early church had a major influence in maintaining the notion that mind, spirit and soul were all closely linked, and to some extent this gave church leaders a certain control over not only the study of the mind but what the mind should think, feel and imagine. The persecution of the witches and the tortures of the Inquisition were justified because the victims of these activities showed obvious signs of deranged minds. Even though Hippocrates in the 5th Century BCE had suggested that epilepsy was a physical disorder, nevertheless many sufferers were subjected to purges, incantations and sacrifices and were seen to be possessed by the Devil. For the church, a healthy mind meant believing in its dogma and an unhealthy mind meant allying oneself with the forces of evil.

It took another two great men to free man from the grip of the church. Leonardo Da Vinci, who insisted on studying the body through dissection and not simply through inference and intuition, described the brain with its hemispheres and ventricles and laid the foundation for modern neuroanatomy. Descartes brought together the principles which established the importance of the mind, separate from the body and the soul. Newton provided the basis for the scientific method by highlighting the power of ration-or-reason, as Aristotle had done

Psychology, Psychiatry, Psychoanalysis

earlier. As a result of their studies, the *dualistic* (separating mind from matter-body), *mechanistic* (regarding the body, including the brain, as a machine) and *reductionistic* (reducing things to their smallest components) modes of thought and behaviour became the prevalent model for the pair of spectacles that have held sway right up until modern times.

From the 17th Century onwards, the study of the mind was in some way over-shadowed by the study of the body. It is not until the late nineteenth and early 20th Century that further steps were taken to understanding the workings of the mind.

Psychoanalysts, Psychologists, Psychiatrists

Psychoanalysts   Followers of Freud, may or may not be medical doctors
Psychologists   Study workings of the mind, not medical doctors
Psychiatrists   Medical doctors treating mental disorders, usually with drugs
Psychotherapists   Medical doctors or non-medical doctors who treat mental disorders without drugs.

Psychoanalysts

Sigmund Freud stands out as one of the great innovators in the study of the mind. He studied medicine and neurology and was initially influenced by Breuer, who used hypnosis to release painful memories in cases of hysteria. Many of the patients Freud saw in Vienna were heavily influenced by the social prohibitions on sexual matters. It appeared to Freud that the painful memories released, first through hypnosis and then through "free association", invariably contained a sexual content.

Freud reintroduced the concept of "energy" into the workings of the mind and labelled this energy "libido". He went on to describe two models of the mind which still form the basis of much psychoanalytic thinking. The first divided the mind into *conscious, preconscious* and *unconscious*. The conscious part of the mind contains all immediately accessible information and memories of present and past experiences. The preconscious contains those memories that, with an effort of will, we can recall, and the unconscious is the repository of all that is forgotten or repressed, and, Freud felt, other painful events. Psychoanalysis is the process by which we can make the unconscious material available to our conscious mind. Freud thought that as long as important events remained unconscious, the mind would remain limited in its capabilities and primate in its behaviour. The second model of the mind included the *ego* (conscious part, aware of the self), *super-ego* (judging critical part influenced by parents, teachers, priests) and *id* (unconscious, childlike, primitive part). Freud saw psychoanalysis as a means of strengthening the *ego* and releasing it from the influences of the *super-ego* and *id* i.e. we have a *higher* self that tells, guides, judges, criticises, leads and directs us; a *middle* self which is the way we operate on an

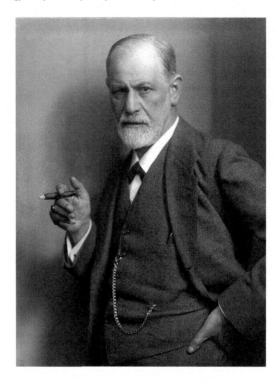

Figure 10.3 Sigmund Freud

everyday practical basis, and a *lower* self which contains our instincts, drives, uncontrolled urges and habit patterns.

The study of the mind therefore was the study of how "Colonel Super-ego", "Lieutenant Ego" and "Private Id" got on together. Freud called the language used by the ego and super-ego "secondary process" and that used by id "primary process", which included the language of dreams, slips of the tongue, free association. Freud felt that the balance between super-ego, ego and id was heavily influenced by the early experiences provided by the parents and that the mind was shaped and moulded by the relationships between father, mother and infant.

Many of Freud's followers have since altered and added to his theories, but his fundamental descriptions of the unconscious elements in the mind still stand as his major achievement and retain their influence to this day. Jung, initially Freud's closest follower, described a very separate area in the workings of the mind. He felt that not only did the mind have a *personal unconscious* as a result of the individual's early experiences, but that the mind was also influenced by *collective* unconscious. By that he meant that the mind had access to and was influenced by all the collective memories of the race, culture, society, nation to which that individual belonged.

Psychology, Psychiatry, Psychoanalysis 143

Freud dismissed this idea as fanciful and unscientific, but again, like Freud's own discoveries, it links well with several older descriptions of the mind.

> Thank God I am Jung and not a Jungian
> – Carl Jung

The fascination we have for myths, legend, folklore, fairy stories, parables and rituals indicate the links between the personal mind and the collective mind. Jung studied these collective experiences and described in detail how he felt the individual mind was shaped by them. He compared these collective experiences in different cultures and was able to identify recurring themes, such as the hero myth (Ulysses, Robin Hood).

Between them Freud and Jung discovered, like the voyagers of old, new territories in the mind, the personal and the collective unconscious.

Behavioural Psychologists

A totally different line of enquiry was followed by the early psychologists who treated the mind as if it were a physical entity, linked entirely to the workings of the brain. This group of psychologists were known as *behavioural psychologists* because they felt the appropriate way to study the mind was to study how it affected the behaviour of the individual. They applied the scientific measuring instruments used in other disciplines to help determine how the mind functioned. They saw the mind as being influenced by "conditioning". The mind responded to a stimulus (food), by a response (eating). The response was either rewarded (hunger assuaged) or punished (feeling sick). Skinner, the most eminent of this group, believed that all behaviour could be explained by the various permutation and combinations of this simple sequence.

The classical experiments by Pavlov illustrated this scientifically; Pavlov rang bells and gave dogs food at the same time. He found that after a while, he would ring the bells and the dogs would salivate even though no food was present.

For Skinner, all phenomena of the mind could be explained through the science of behaviourism, and in the most extreme form of this theory he maintained that "free will" was an illusion described by idealists who refused to accept the proofs of his discoveries. Behavioural psychology has led to treating mental disturbances as if they were inappropriate conditioned responses. If you are afraid of flying, the mental response to entering an airplane has nothing to do with your past early experience or, if they do, it is irrelevant to subsequent treatment. The individual with a fear is gradually introduced to the stimulus (airplane) and is rewarded every time he is able to reduce his fear or punished if his response is "wrong". Behavioural psychologists introduced a new and important dimension to the study of the mind which appeared to be in total opposition to that of the analysts, and certainly their methods of treating mental disorders were very different.

Figure 10.4 Ivan Pavlov

Humanistic Psychologists

The next group of psychologists who studied the mind were the *humanistic psychologists*. This group felt that it was unhelpful to reduce the mind to the Freudian mental structure of super-ego, ego and id, or the experimental processes of operant conditioning described by Skinner and his followers. They felt these "models" somehow did not describe the essential experience of being human. They looked to existential philosophers for their inspiration. Maslow, a major writer in this area, outlined the need the mind has for reaching its full potential through creative acts.

Humanistic psychologists studied the workings of the mind by studying especially creative or gifted people. They emphasised the healthy aspects of the mind and laid the foundation to the "positive thinking" school. Think positively and you will behave positively. They emphasised the strength of the conscious mind and its ability to overcome the *unconscious* influences. Therapists trained in this model of the mind limit the exploration of "unconscious tendencies" and do not expose their clients to controlled behaviour modifications. They tend to focus on the enhancement of the individual's emotional life and reinforce the positive

Psychology, Psychiatry, Psychoanalysis 145

and healthy tendencies already present. They focus on the "here and now" rather than the past or future.

MASLOW'S HIERARCHY OF NEEDS

*I've recently perused the work of **Maslow**,*
who's well-known for his quite perceptive claims:
he says the needs that every person has go
from basic ones like food to higher aims.
*The **Physiological** needs come first – survival*
requires us to eat, to drink, to sleep.
*When those are met, then **Safety** starts to rival*
them for attention, since we have a deep
*desire to be protected. Then comes **Love***
*and **Belonging**: we need family and friends*
to stave off loneliness. And then above
*this stage, there's self-**Esteem**. Our health depends*
on these four all being met, so motivation
*impels us to **Self-actualisation**.*

Thomas X. Ling[10]

Psychiatrists

Psychiatrists who use drugs or ECT (electroconvulsive therapy, which is electrical stimulation of the brain) to manage mental disorders see the mind like the behaviourists, as a function of the brain. The brain is like other organs in the body and can be studied using the instruments that doctors have used to study other organs. They have been influenced therefore by the neuroanatomists and neurophysiologists who have studied the brain and the mind with increasing success in the last twenty to thirty years.

For centuries, men have drilled holes in the skull, probed and explored the brain using surgical and, more recently, electrical instruments. In the last thirty years, brain surgeons have severed connections in the brain in an attempt to cure epilepsy and portions of the brain have been removed to treat personality disorders.

In more recent years, the electroencephalograph (EEG) has been used to measure electrical activity arising from the brain and, as with a jigsaw puzzle, the link between the anatomical parts of the brain and its functions is slowly being discovered. For the purposes of this book we shall limit ourselves to a description of the mental functions of the brain and the way they influence our daily life. The major part of the brain is made up of two hemispheres joined by millions of neurons (nerve cells with long connecting threads). The left hemisphere controls the movement on the right side of the body and the right hemisphere controls the left side of the body. In addition, the left hemisphere governs

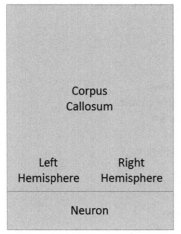

Figure 10.5 The Hemispheres of the Brain

those functions principally to do with speech, rational thought, logical reasoning, objective analysis, whilst the right hemisphere is concerned with how things relate to one another.

The right hemisphere recognises shapes, patterns and images, and it covers our intuitive sense. It appears that each hemisphere can function independently of the other, but that in most people one hemisphere plays a more dominant role. For most people the left hemisphere is the dominant hemisphere, resulting in more right-handed people. Not only does the dominant hemisphere govern the movement and handedness but it seems to determine the prevailing "consciousness" or mode of thought.

Neuroscience, Neuroimaging and Neurotransmitters

There has been an enormous advance in the understanding of brain structures and brain functioning with the development of brain imagining techniques. This has allowed researchers and brain surgeons to pinpoint both anatomical disorders e.g. brain tumours, as well as the location of how the brain functions. Magnetic resonance imagining (MRI) allows us to be more precise as to which part of the brain "lights up" when we perform separate tasks from reading, sleeping, dreaming – and experiencing emotions (e.g. anger, compassion, memory recall etc.). These mapping techniques are still in their infancy, and caution needs to be applied that sometimes is not heeded in the articles found in more popular journals. What most brain researchers agree on is that there is a degree of "plasticity" in the functions of different parts of the brain. Another model – the "triune brain", first described by Paul MacLean and made popular by Carl Sagan in his ground-breaking book *The Dragons of Eden*,[11] is no longer considered to be as definite as first described. Nevertheless, it provides a helpful description of the evolution of the mammalian brain – the model suggests the following:

Reptilian brain   – governing our basic instinct
Limbic system   – governing our emotional and expressive behaviour
Frontal cortex   – governing our thoughts, language, judgement

Section 3: Linking Biography with Academic Literature

1. I believe Bowlby's attachment theory allows me to understand how and why I have never felt, until recently, that I possess a "secure base".

As Bowlby writes,

> Attachment behaviour . . . is a form of instinctive behaviour that develops in humans, as in other mammals, during infancy, and has as its aim or goal/ proximity to a mother-figure. The function of attachment behaviour, as suggested, is protection from predators. Whilst attachment behaviour is shown especially strongly during childhood when it is directed towards parent figures, it none the less continues to be active during adult life when it is usually directed towards some active and dominant figure, often a relative but sometimes an employer or some elder of the community. Attachment behaviour, the theory emphasises, is elicited when a person (child or adult) is sick or in trouble, and is elicited at high intensity when he is frightened or when the attachment-figure cannot be found. Because, in the light of this theory, attachment behaviour is regarded as a normal and healthy part of man's instinctive makeup, it is held to be most misleading to term it 'regressive' or childish when seen in an older child or adult. For this reason, too, the term 'dependency' is regarded as leading to a seriously mistaken perspective, for in everyday speech to describe someone as dependent cannot help carrying with it overtones of criticism. By contrast, to describe someone as attached carries with it a positive evaluation.[12]

This failure of not having a secure base may explain my "nomadic" existence, which I only began to accept after meeting Gideon Ben Barrak. It may also explain, partly, my marriage's breakdown; "I never felt safe". It certainly explains my near "breakdown" when my first girlfriend jilted me when I was

148 *Psychology, Psychiatry, Psychoanalysis*

16 years old. And it also explains my need to build sheds where I can feel safe and, finally, I have learnt to create a series of attachment figures by always having a list of three "wise men" and three "wise women" to turn to.

2. I am sure there are other possible and probable explanations using examples of other psychodynamic theory; phrases such as puer aeternus; narcissism, trickster and Napoleon complex, but I think I will stick with Bowlby, and although I cannot turn him into a Babushka doll, I am sure one of my earliest "dolls" is a young infant craving for maternal contact. I have spent many years of my life following a sequence of different "pied pipers" that eventually I have also allowed myself to become one – with what success is uncertain, and failures there are many.
3. I have selected in my eighth and ninth decade and become a disciple of the Stoics, writing a daily diary and consuming the writings of Zeno, Epictetus, Marcus Aurelius and Seneca.
4. I expand on this on this on the final chapter.

Notes

1 P. Agarwal (2020). *Sway: Unravelling Unconscious Bias*. London. Bloomsbury.
2 Agarwal (2020). *Ibid*.
3 Agarwal (2020). *Ibid*.
4 J. Bowlby (1988). *A Secure Base*. Abingdon. Routledge.
5 I. Turgenev (1978. First published 1860). *First Love*. London. Penguin Classics.
6 M. Balint (2000. First published 1957). *The Doctor, His Patient, and His Illness*. London. Churchill Livingstone.
7 M. Marinker (1972). A Teachers' Workshop. *The Journal of the Royal College of General Practitioners* 22(121). pp. 551–559.
8 P. Freeling & S. Barry (1982). *In-service Training: Study of the Nuffield Courses of the Royal College of General Practitioners*. Abingdon. Routledge.
9 P. S. Byrne & B. E. L. Long (1976). *Doctors Talking to Patients: A Study of the Verbal Behaviour of General Practitioners Consulting in Their Surgeries*. London. HMSO.
10 Thomas X. Ling (2012). *Maslow's Hierarchy of Needs*. Available at https://allpoetry.com/poem/9501557-Maslows-Hierarchy-of-Needs-by-Discoveria. Last accessed July 2022.
11 C. Sagan (1978). *The Dragons of Eden: Speculations on the Evolution of Human Intelligence*. New York. Random House.
12 Bowlby (1988). *Op. Cit*.

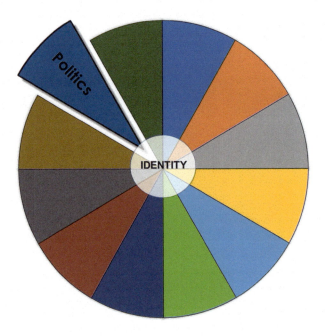

Figure 11.0

11 Politics, Philosophy

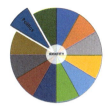

Figure 11.0

Section 1: Biography

I have never taken any classes in politics or philosophy. I can only claim to have acquired, what I consider as my politics "identity", through my reading newspapers, books and discussions mostly with like-minded friends. I was able to vote for all the general elections in the UK from my arrival in England in 1960. I have lived under the premierships of Harold Macmillan; Sir Alec Douglas-Home; Harold Wilson (twice); Edward Heath; James Callaghan; Margaret Thatcher; John Major; Tony Blair; Gordon Brown; David Cameron; Theresa May and Boris Johnson. Eight conservative and four (five, if you count Harold Wilson twice) labour. My earliest political memory was the death of Winston Churchill in 1965. I remember this date because my father, then aged 60, took the day off and queued outside Westminster Abbey all day to pay his respects.

As with religion, we never discussed politics around the dining room table, and I cannot recollect any serious discussions with my father, who I know voted conservative when he became eligible to do so.

I had, by then, attended "Ban the Bomb" marches in London and had begun to "follow" the leadership of Michael Foot and Tony Benn. When Harold Wilson became Prime Minster, it felt like a big page-turner in my political life, but not as great as when Tony Blair defeated John Major. I remember staying up all night and feeling as if our whole world would change, which it did (for a while). It has never crossed my mind to join the Labour, or the Liberal political party, and although holding strong views, it has not propelled me to become practically involved in politics. All my friends were "of the left", as were, I suspect, my brothers, though possibly not the eldest. Like many citizens of the UK, I find our current prime minister a dangerous fool and a fraud, and have little or no respect for him, whereas I could respect several of the Conservative party ministers, even though I may not have agreed with them.

Living in America, as I now do for a large proportion of the year, I fear for the future of democracy, which was never in jeopardy before the emergence of Donald Trump, and which does not argue well, given the challenges we now face.

DOI: 10.4324/9781003401414-12

152   *Politics, Philosophy*

I attach the *Letter from America* I sent to my grandchildren in August 2021 in which I summarise the challenges the human species face, and which it appears, not willing to address seriously enough.

I find myself preoccupied with what I now label, "our seven deadly challenges". I list them hereafter and will attempt to share with you my own responses to their challenges:

8. Climate change
9. The Afghanistan debacle
10. Covid revisited – what is the next pandemic?
11. Issues of race, ethnicity and voting rights
12. Artificial intelligence and the loss of meaning
13. The fault line in the Enlightenment
14. Toxic masculinity

Firstly, let me say that my generation i.e. those of us born in the 1940's, are largely responsible for the majority of these challenges, and your generation (all aged in your 20's and younger) are likely to be most affected by them. I generally write only two A4 pages in these letters, and it would take me at least two pages to outline how I see each of these challenges. I will try to limit myself around 100–200 words for each and will expand in future letters, as I feel able to.

1. Climate change
    These last few weeks and months have seen an acceleration of uncontrollable fires in the USA, Greece, Germany and Bangladesh, never experienced before. Overwhelming floods in Haiti, Florida, Germany and China, as well as dwindling water levels in some of our larger lakes and rivers – Colorado, Arizona, Canada and Africa. The melting of the Northern Icebergs has led to a drop in the temperature of the Gulf Stream, effecting the East coast of the United States. Rain has fallen on the Arctic for the first time.
2. The Afghanistan debacle
    The rapid (11 days) surrender of the Afghanistan government and the surrender of the army (trained by the US and NATO) has led to the horror currently occurring in the International Airport at Kabul. The airport is mobbed by the desperate and afraid, and is at the mercy of almost certain attack by the Taliban when they decide so to do. The calamitous response by the Biden government includes the fact that there was no planning or discussion with other Western nations (UK, Poland, France, Germany – NATO), who also had embassies, troupes and "loyal" Afghanistan folk. The consequences for the Western alliance are dire. The only bargaining

chip the US still has is that it can block the 16 billion dollars of Afghanistan money it holds in US banks.

3. Covid revisited

It is clear we have not got on top of this pandemic, neither in Western countries, let alone in India, China or worse still, Africa. Why is South Africa selling their vaccine abroad rather than ensuring its own population is vaccinated? I wrote an article on pandemics, and labelled it, using Pasteur's last words, "The Bacteria is nothing, the terrain is everything". In other words, unless we address the inequality that exists i.e. nutrition, housing, education, health and wealth, pandemics will continue to occur.

4. Issues of race, ethnicity and voting rights

We have seen both during and post the Trump presidency a determined attempt by many Republican States to alter voting processes in order to limit the number of non-White voters. Social European countries are also changing their laws governing voting (Hungary, Poland, Turkey) by limiting citizenship voting rights to immigrants (MAGA – Make America Great Again, really means MAWA – Make America White Again).

5. Artificial intelligence and the loss of meaning

Irakli Beridze, Head of the Centre for Artificial Intelligence and Robotics at UNICRI, United Nations, has expressed:

I think the dangerous applications for AI, from my point of view would be criminals or large terrorist organizations using it to disrupt large processes or simply do pure harm. [Terrorists could cause harm] via digital warfare, or it could be a combination of robotics, drones, with AI and other things as well that could be really dangerous. And, of course, other risks come from things like job losses. If we have massive numbers of people losing jobs and don't find a solution it will be extremely dangerous. Things like lethal autonomous weapons systems should be properly governed – otherwise there's massive potential of misuse. (https://futurism. com/artificial-intelligence-experts-fear)

Devaluation of humanity; Joseph Weizenbaum wrote that AI applications cannot, by definition, successfully simulate genuine human empathy, and that the use of AI technology in fields such as customer service or psychotherapy was deeply misguided. Weizenbaum was also bothered that AI researchers (and some philosophers) were willing to view the human mind as nothing more than a computer program (a position that is now known as computationalism). To Weizenbaum these points suggest that AI research devalues human life. (https://en.wikipedia.org/wiki/ Artificial_intelligence)

6. The fault line in the Enlightenment

I make no apologies for using this summing up to place the preceding sections against the background of three centuries of Western thought and culture encapsulated by what we have known as The Enlightenment.

154 *Politics, Philosophy*

Vickers (1968/2001), predominantly, but Engel (1980), Schon (1983; 1987), and others recognised the fault lines in The Enlightenment which persist to this day and are currently helping to create the geo-political turmoil that we seem incapable of addressing. Vickers was able to escape from the rigidity of his Victorian upper-middle-class background, embrace systems theory and address the limitations of science-based epistemology bound by a 17th-century worldview. His challenge to the direction of professionalism in medicine at least was based on his own abiding concern for the importance of human rather than technological values and of ethical judgments.

Gertrude Himmelfarb (2005) in her book, "The Roads to Modernity: the British, French and American Enlightenments", provides a scholarly exposition on these "fault-lines". The French Enlightenment driving the ideology of reason, the British – the sociology of virtue and the Americans the emphasis on politics of liberty. All three have both influenced and driven modern Western culture and education to be what it is today. However, the competing "models" of enlightenment have resulted in a diminution of the centrality of the golden rule: that one should treat others as one wishes to be treated oneself as found in all major world religions. (Boyett, 2016; Coles, 2015).

7. Toxic masculinity

In summary, I would say that there is now general acceptance that the concept of toxic masculinity is real, and includes many of the following traits: risk taking; violence; need for emotional control; dominance; desire to win; pursuit of social status; the emphasis on toughness; dominance leading to sexual assault; rage and domestic violence.

Critiques of the term "toxic masculinity" argue that the traits linked to the term are not inherently wrong or harmful and are often also linked to courage, leadership, bravery and self-reliance.

Where there is even more argument is whether the traits associated with toxic masculinity are the product of genetic, hormonal, biological or psychological factors or whether the social family cultural expectations of "what it is to be a man" result in learned behaviours passed from father to son, as in "boys will be boys".

I find the term "fragile masculinity" to be a more helpful concept and allows for the split between traditional accepted standards of masculinity and femininity to be not necessarily linked to gender i.e. we all can have masculine and feminine traits.

I suspect, and believe, that toxic masculinity may well be the cause of the issues outlined in 1–6. It requires a much longer paper to explain why.

I would be interested to hear from you with regard to the issue raised by this letter.

Section 2: Academic Literature

A selection of political theory through the ages.

The Greek Originators – Plato/Aristotle, Socrates/Alexander

The word *polis* is Greek for the city, and it was Plato who first elaborated the purpose of government, and his book, "*The Republic*" (375 BC) sets the stage for what was to follow. The book reads as a series of conversations between Plato and Socrates, and his famous metaphor of the cave underpinned his view that Kings and Princes ruled the Cities. Human beings remain trapped in the cave (facing the wall, and only experiencing the World through the shadows cast on the wall from the caves entrance). He thus established the rule by one man, not chosen by the populace. So, no democracy yet, but rule of law yes, as determined by the King/Prince who could be supported by a national council and curators of law.

Aristotle disagreed with Plato's model but supported the idea that man was different from other animals and was a political animal; by that he meant he was equipped from birth with intelligence and moral qualities. It is important to remember that slaves were never to be granted citizenship and were

Figure 11.1 Plato Quote

156   *Politics, Philosophy*

considered slaves by nature. Plato, Socrates and Aristotle saw the city state (the Polis) as the basis for civilisation. This fact could no longer be held when Alexander the Great conquered most of the Eastern Mediterranean and created a vast Empire. This new entity will have contained several Cities, States, Polis that by no means covered the large population which now lived in a vast Empire.

The Roman Empire to follow included most of the lands of the Greek Empire but also most of Western Europe as well as most of England.

Marcus Aurelius (121 AD-180 AD) was one of the five Good Emperors. The others were Antoninus Pius, Nerva, Trajan, and Hadrian. Marcus was also known as the Philosopher Emperor and considered himself a Stoic, writing a diary which became known as *Meditations*.[1]

Cicero was of great influence on Marcus and we begin to see what would later become known as "moral sentiments" creep into the political "bible". Cicero wrote the purpose of Government was to,

Make human life better by our thoughts and efforts.[2]

Constantine converted to Christianity in 312 AD and it became the sole religion throughout the Holy Roman Empire. St. Augustine's *City of God,* written in 413 AD, forms the beginning of how the Christian Church became the only acceptable spiritual authority. This would determine both the structure (Divine Right of Kings) and the laws (Ten Commandments) that constituted the laws of Government.

The Pope in Rome together with the Holy Roman Emperor were the dominant players for a few centuries. It was not until Machiavelli (1469–1527) wrote his famous book, *"The Prince"*, [2] that the secularisation of political philosophy could be said to begin. His views of mankind were not those of a religious despot. He wrote,

Since the desire of men are insatiable, nature prompting them to desire all things and fortune permitting them to enjoy but few, there results a constant discontent in their minds, and a loathing of what they possess.

He continues,

The Prince must combine the strength of the lion with the cunning of the fox. For men ought to be either well treated or crushed, because they can avenge themselves of lighter injuries, of more serious ones they cannot. Moreover, irresolute princes who follow a neutral path are generally ruined.[3]

Machiavelli did believe in "the end justifies the means".

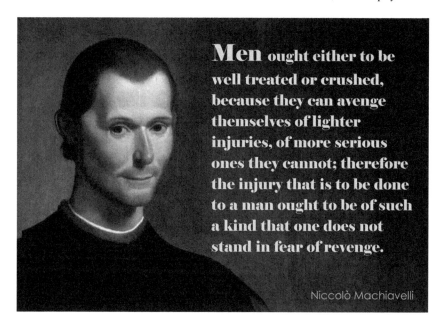

Figure 11.2 Machiavelli Quote

We can jump a century or two and begin to outline the emergence of modern political theory and ideology. These include:

1. Liberalism
2. Marxism
3. Socialism
4. Anarchism
5. Conservatism
6. Totalitarianism

Liberalism

From the word, *Liber* – being free. Liberalism has been the predominant political approach for the majority of European democracies and formed the foundation of the American Constitution. It is linked to the Age of Enlightenment.

By that time, Copernicus, the astronomer, had bravely published his life's work and put the sun at the centre of the universe, thus displacing the earth from its central position in the heavens. Galileo, who followed him, set about proving the brilliance of Copernicus' deductions, doing so with the aid of

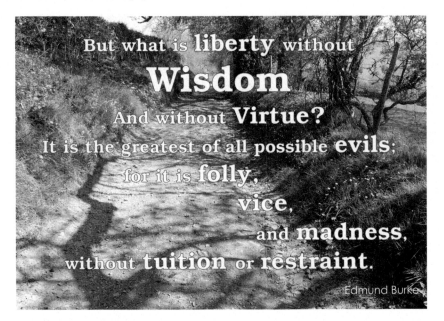

Figure 11.3 Edmund Burke Quote

a giant telescope. So incensed were the elders of the Church of this 'blasphemous' behaviour that Galileo was arrested and under pressure, recanted. The earth, however, did not return to the center of the heavens and this progress in understanding ourselves and our world was unstoppable. The separation of religion from science had begun and was firmly encouraged by two other great scientists, Isaac Newton and Rene Descartes. Newton's view of the universe was governed by _reason_ – all events took place as a result of mathematical laws which were determined by the principle law of cause and effect. He pointed out that gods and spirits had nothing to do with why we developed disease.[4,5]

Thomas Hobbes, John Locke, and Edmund Burke are seen as some of the first architects of this moral philosophy. In France, Montaigne, Rousseau and Voltaire emphasised the social, as opposed to the individual, aspects of liberalism. It was Jeremy Bentham who established the concept of Utilitarianism (*the greatest happiness for the greatest number*) and John Rawls who added the concept of fairness and justice in his book, "*Political Liberalism*".[6] Economics (Adam Smith) and the Free Market (Freidman von Hayek) all claimed the word "liberalism" as well. So Liberalism as a political concept can be seen as a coat hanger on which different ideas and functions are mixed in with different ideologies.

Socialism

I find it helpful to view Socialism as a family of 'isms, including Marxism, Communism and Anarchism. More recently and starting in the Nordic countries, the word Democratic is added to the word Social, as it was for a short period in the UK Social-Democratic Party (SDP). The word Socialism is derived from the Latin word *Socire* meaning to share. It was used and still is to emphasise the opposite of the individualism which underpins the previous Liberalism and Capitalism.

Socialist theory emphasises that "it is the economic structure of society that helps to determine whether a society operates in an ethical, moral and just manner". It is the emphasis in sharing the collective, economic framework that will allow for the four basic tenets as describe by Berki:[7] egalitarianism, moralism, rationalism and libertarianism.

Its roots in England go back to Levelers (post the revolution 17th Century) and also draws on the early Christian traditions, which formed the basis of both the Methodist and Utilitarian movement. Liberation theology, which arose in the Latin American Roman Catholic Church in the 1960s, was based on socialist ideology. The Nordic countries adopted the term Democratic Socialism to emphasise the difference from the totalitarian models of Socialism which were present in both Marxism and Communism.

The following two quotations may help to put Socialism in historical context and in its relationship to Liberalism and Capitalism.

It really is impossible to understand either the French revolution or the early socialists unless one possesses some awareness of the challenge which the new liberal individualism represented to older ways of life.[8]

Socialism began a revolt against capitalism and its conception of man and society was initially developed as an alternative to the one which in the socialist view underlay and reinforced capitalist society.[9]

Barbara Goodwin in her excellent short book *Using Political Ideas* summarises the Nucleus of Socialism philosophy as follows:

The concern for poverty
A class analysis of society
Egalitarianism
Communal ownership or the means of production
Popular sovereignty
"Subordination of the individual to society"
Human creativity and sociability
The virtues of co-operation
Idealization of work as unalienated labour
Freedom as fulfilment
Internationalism[10]

160 *Politics, Philosophy*

Critiques of Socialism all too often make the link with Marxism and Communism in order to underpin its totalitarian tendencies. In 1989 the 18th Congress of Socialist International adopted a new Declaration of Principles:

> Democratic socialism is an international movement for freedom, social justice, and solidarity. Its goal is to achieve a peaceful world where these basic values can be enhanced and where each individual can live a meaningful life with the full development of his or her personality and talents, and with the guarantee of human and civil rights in a democratic framework of society.[11]

Further changes to the concept of Socialism were introduced by Tony Blair, the Leader of the Labour Party in the UK in the 1990s. "The Third Way", as it was labelled, stated:

> The Labour Party is a democratic socialist party. It believes that, by the strength of our common endeavour we achieve more than we achieve alone, so as to create for each of us, the means to realise our true potential, and, for all of us a community in which power, wealth, and opportunity are in the hands of the many, not the few.[12]

Conservatism

Embodies a commitment to an ideology and mentality rather than focus on an outcome. Indeed the outcome of a conservative ideology is very different in the UK than it is in Iran, for instance. So there can be, and there are, very different forms of Conservatism e.g. Liberal Conservatism, Progressive Conservatism, Religious Conservatism, Authoritarian Conservatism. The tenets of this ideology emphasise tradition, continuity, hierarchy, authority and preservation of religious organisations. Conservatives will respond negatively to change and emphasise the importance of traditional, moral codes, social norms and property rights.

Edmund Burke (influenced by the horror of the French Revolution) is seen as the "father" of Conservatism as it developed in the UK and US. He wrote:

> It is with infinite caution that any man ought to venture upon pulling down an edifice which has answered in any tolerable degree for ages the common purpose of society.[13]

One of the important features of Conservatism is the belief in "human imperfectability". This leads to the support for strong, and at times authoritarian, government. The role of such governments is to uphold the law, to police the streets, punish the wicked and imprison the guilty. Such governments should protect rights of law abiding citizens and not interfere with the freedom of those who pursue their own destiny. This form of Liberal Conservatism is found both in the

Politics, Philosophy 161

UK and the US. In the US, the freedom to bear arms and defend one's property is considered a constitutional right.

The Thatcher Government in the UK encouraged the sale of "social housing" and adopted a laissez-faire economic policy that are the hallmarks of Capitalism (outlined in the next section).

Another important "pillar" of this form of Conservatism is the acceptance of the permanence of a hierarchical social system – "The poor will always be with us", or as Charles Dickens so elegantly wrote in *"The Chimes"*,

O let us love our occupations,
Bless the squire and his relations,
Live upon our daily rations,
And always know our proper stations.[14]

It is important to acknowledge that social hierarchical systems are found East/West, North/South. The most ingrained and widespread is in India (Hindu social organisation).

The strong desire for "no change" and stability leads to the centrality of national identity and the in-group/out-group phenomenon we have observed as a result of President Trump's "Make America Great Again" (MAGA) which is not too distant from the desire to "Make America White Again".

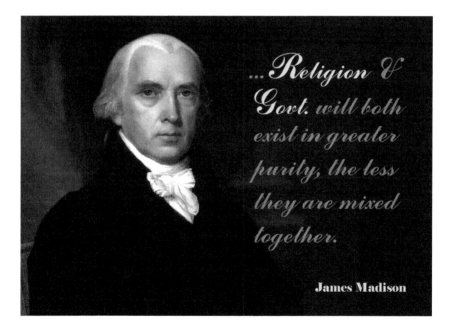

Figure 11.4 James Madison Quote

162 *Politics, Philosophy*

The emphasis on individual freedom, individual responsibility, "small government", low taxes leads to reducing the government involvement in the Welfare State and maximises individual philanthropy and charitable donations (from those who have to those who have not). The unintended consequence of this policy is to embed the social hierarchy as a permanent feature in the country.

Following the crash in 2008 and the current pandemic crisis we cannot avoid (even if we wanted to) that we are living through an existential crisis, and we have not even mentioned the issue of Climate Change.

This has not passed unnoticed by an avalanche of authors. I list hereafter a small selection of those I chose to read in preparation for this short volume!

1. And The Weak Suffer What They Must? — Yaris Varoufakis[15]
2. The State We're In — Will Hutton[16]
3. The Ascent Of Money — Niall Ferguson[17]
4. Post Capitalism: A Guide to our Future — Paul Mason[18]
5. The Crisis Of Global Capitalism: Open Society Endangered — George Soros[19]
6. The State We Need — Michael Meacher[20]
7. What Money Can't Buy — Michael J Sandel[21]
8. The Fourth Revolution — Adrian Wooldridge & John Micklethwait[22]
9. The Body Economic: Why Austerity Kills — David Stuckler and Sanjay Basu[23]
10. Progressive Capitalism: How to Achieve Economic Growth, Liberty & Social Justice — David Sainsbury[24]
11. Winners Take All: The Elite Charade of Changing the World — Anand Giridharadas[25]
12. I Spend Therefore I Am: How Economics Has Changed the Way We Think & Feel — Philip Roscoe[26]
13. Hope Without Optimism — Terry Eagleton[27]

Section 3: Linking Biography with Academic Literature

So, how can I in this final section try and summarise what these experts offer? I obviously cannot. What I can do is point out that in only one of these excellent texts does the word compassion appear in the references. So, yes, I have something to add.

It would be fair to say that there was mention of "moral sentiments" and the "greatest happiness for the greatest number", but no specific problems were identified, and no specific solutions were offered. We now must introduce the Five Giants that have been identified and require attention if the talk of moral sentiments, happiness, justice are not to be just words.

The Five Giants

The book *The Five Giants*,[28] written by Nicholas Timmins (Harper Collins 1995), is a biography of the emergence of the Welfare State in the United Kingdom. The Beveridge Report, as it came to be known, was written at the instigation of the UK War Cabinet in 1942 and implemented by the Labour Government when it won the post-war election in 1945.

The Five Giants that Beveridge identified were: Want; Disease; Ignorance; Squalor, and Idleness. I have selected some of the brief advisory notes sent to the Government on 25 June 1942.

Extract from notes from the advisory panel on Home Affairs on Reconstruction Problems: the Five Giants on the Road, 25 June 1942 (T 161/1165)

Assuming victory for the United Nations, is there any good reason for doubting our capacity after this war to do what was well within our reach just before it? We shall be poorer in the immediate aftermath of war, by loss of investments and in other ways. We shall not be able to afford so much waste or slackness. But need we, even in the immediate aftermath of war, be very much poorer than in 1936? And need we stay poorer for any length of time? Technical progress will not stop. To be afraid of the Giant Want is senseless cowardice.

Abolition of want in the sense in which that word is used here does not mean satisfying all desires. The extent to which the standard of living can be kept above the national minimum depends upon the degree of success achieved in dealing with the fifth giant: Idleness.

1. Disease: Attack on disease is a matter of prevention; second of cure. Prevention, beginning with health services in the narrow sense, spreads outwards into the problem of sanitation, housing, nutrition and local government. As to cure, opinion both public and professional, is probably ripe for a general re-organisation of the medical service of the community- so as to ensure that the best science of the community- so as to ensure that the best that science can do is available for the treatment of every citizen at home and in institutions, irrespective of his personal means. There are practical difficulties and sectional interests to be overcome in this field as in dealing with want, but no fundamental political issues.

2. Ignorance: Successful attack on Ignorance is a condition of good government under democracy. It is the only way of combining the efficiency of a dictatorship with the essential freedom of the citizen. Attack on Ignorance like attack on Want raises no fundamental political issues, and touches fewer vested interests. Progress on this line should be easy. But attack on Ignorance is not simply or mainly a question of raising the school age or widening the

164 *Politics, Philosophy*

educational ladder to higher schools and Universities. It is a question at least as much of adult education on an immense scale. That in turn means both getting more leisure and giving guidance in using leisure well.

3. Squalor: The irresistible disorderly growth of great cities, which may be described in one word as conurbation, is almost as great a social evil as unemployment. It has involved in the past daily waste of life and human energy in needless travel, bad housing and ill health, needless exhausting toil for the housewife in struggling with dirt and discomfort, habituation of the population to hideous surroundings. Co-urbation is a phenomenon as universal as unemployment- an inseparable accompaniment hitherto of private enterprise and private ownership of land. The only effective remedy is control of the distribution of industry, – control not persuasion, for population goes where industry calls for it. Distribution of industry in turn involves control of the use of land, imaginative centralised direction of transport and public utilities, and re-organisation of local government. Here is a giant indeed.

4. Idleness: Want of the means subsistence could be abolished by a policy of the national minimum, as outlined above. But abolition of Want is an inadequate aim. Public opinion will demand that with income security shall go a reasonable opportunity of productive work, not indeed with absolute continuity of jobs, but with more jobs than idleness for everyone. It will demand standards of living far above the minimum of physical subsistence. The policy of a national minimum must be combined with a policy of maintaining productive employment, of ensuring that the productive resources of the country are used to meet the needs of the people.

Next to the maintenance of peace, maintenance of productive employment is the most important of all reconstruction aims. It is the most important in itself; if the Giant of Idleness can be destroyed, all the aims of reconstruction come within reach; if not, they are out.

CONCLUSION

The five giants are of an increasing order of strength and ferocity. Attacks on Want, Disease and Ignorance all affect sectional interests but raise no fundamental political issues. The task of framing these attacks is already to some extent in hand in regard to Want by the Inter-Departmental Committee on Social Insurance and Allied Services, in regard to Disease by the Ministry of Health and by that Committee, in regard to Ignorance by the Board of Education.

In regard to the two remaining giants the position is different. It is difficult to see how attacks on Squalor and Idleness could be pressed home by a Government which had not made up its mind for State planning, for some form of nationalisation of land or at least of land values, and for nationalisation of certain essential services. In other words attacks on Squalor and Idleness do raise what have been regarded as hitherto political issues. Whether they must

Politics, Philosophy 165

continue to be so regarded, can be determined best by considering actual plans for maintaining productive employment and for distributing industry and population so as to prevent con-urbation and squalor. The making of such plans calls for the setting up of an Economic General Staff, which means neither a Committee of Ministers, nor a Committee of departmental officials, nor an Advisory panel, nor the Treasury or Board of Trade. It means, in fact, an Economic General Staff. It means an organ of Government which does not yet exist, with an access to the minds of decisive Ministers which has not yet been provided.[29]

As a foot note, I'd like to add these words from the Dalai Lama:

Love and compassion are necessities, not luxuries; without them, humanity cannot survive.[30]

I finish with two poems, one short and one longer; the short one is written by myself and the longer one written by William Shakespeare, that for me stands as a testament to where we have been, where we are and where we should go with compassion.

Compassion and the Other

It is in the safety of
my own quiet corner
that I can acknowledge
my own shadow

Filled as it is with
all the blocks and hurdles
that limit my capacity
for compassion
to the other.
My shadow is my own other.

Know it
befriend it
you will find it
possible
to approach all the others
you will meet
on your own
journey
with compassion.
                    Patrick Pietroni[31]

166 *Politics, Philosophy*

To be, or not to be, that is the question

To be, or not to be, that is the question:
Whether 'tis nobler in the mind to suffer
The slings and arrows of outrageous fortune,
Or to take arms against a sea of troubles
And by opposing end them. To die – to sleep,
No more; and by a sleep to say we end
The heart-ache and the thousand natural shocks
That flesh is heir to: 'tis a consummation
Devoutly to be wish'd. To die, to sleep;
To sleep, perchance to dream – ay, there's the rub:
For in that sleep of death what dreams may come,
When we have shuffled off this mortal coil,
Must give us pause – there's the respect
That makes calamity of so long life.
For who would bear the whips and scorns of time,
Th'oppressor's wrong, the proud man's contumely,
The pangs of dispriz'd love, the law's delay,
The insolence of office, and the spurns
That patient merit of th'unworthy takes,
When he himself might his quietus make
With a bare bodkin? Who would fardels bear,
To grunt and sweat under a weary life,
But that the dread of something after death,
The undiscovere'd country, from whose bourn
No traveller returns, puzzles the will,
And makes us rather bear those ills we have
Than fly to others that we know not of?
Thus conscience doth make cowards of us all,
And thus the native hue of resolution
Is sicklied o'er with the pale cast of thought,

And enterprises of great pith and moment
With this regard their currents turn awry
And lose the name of action.

William Shakespeare[32]

Notes

1 M. Aurelius (1952). *The Meditations of Marcus Aurelius Antoninus*. Chicago. University of Chicago.
2 M. T. Cicero & W. Melmoth (Trans.). (1889). *Old Age and Friendship*. Cassell's National Library no. 195.

Politics, Philosophy 167

3 N. Machiavelli (2010. First published 1532). *The Prince*. Glasgow. SoHo Books.
4 N. Machiavelli (2010. First published 1532). *Ibid*.
5 P. Pietroni (1990). *The Greening of Medicine*. London. Victor Gollancz.
6 J. Rawls (1993). *Political Liberalism*. New York. Columbia University Press.
7 R. N. Berki (1975). *Socialism*. London. J.M. Dent.
8 G. Lichtheim (1969). *The Origins of Socialism*. London. Weidenfeld & Nicholson.
9 B. Parekh (Ed.) (1975). *The Concept of Socialism*. London. Croom Helm.
10 B. Goodwin (1982., 2nd ed). *Using Political Ideas*. London. Wiley & Sons.
11 Progressive Politics for a Fairer World (2008). *Socialist International*. Available at: www.socialistinternational.org/. Last accessed: July 2022.
12 Labour Party Clause IV (2008). Available at: https://en.m.wikipedia.org/wiki/Clause_IV. Last accessed: July 2022.
13 Goodwin (1982., 2nd ed). *Op. Cit.*
14 C. Dickens (1844). *The Chimes*. London. Chapman & Hall.
15 Y. Varoufakis (2016). *And the Weak Suffer What They Must?* London. Penguin Random House.
16 W. Hutton (1995). *The State We're In*. New York. Random House.
17 N. Ferguson (2009). *The Ascent of Money*. London. Penguin.
18 P. Mason (2015). *Post Capitalism: A Guide to our Future*. London. Allen Lane.
19 G. Soros (1998). *The Crisis of Global Capitalism: Open Society Endangered*. London. Little, Brown Book Group.
20 M. Meacher (2013). *The State We Need*. London. Biteback Publishing.
21 M. J. Sandel (2012). *What Money Can't Buy*. London. Penguin.
22 A. Woodlridge & J. Micklethwait (2014). *The Fourth Revolution*. London. Allen Lane.
23 D. Stuckler & S. Basu (2013). *The Body Economic: Why Austerity Kills*. London. Allen Lane.
24 D. Sainsbury (2013). *Progressive Capitalism: How to Achieve Economic Growth, Liberty & Social Justice*. London. Biteback Publishing.
25 A. Giridharadas (2018). *Winners Take All: The Elite Charade of Changing the World*. New York. Alfred A Knopf.
26 P. Roscoe (2014). *I Spend Therefore I Am: How Economics Has Changed the Way We Think & Feel*. London. Viking Penguin.
27 T. Eagleton (2015). *Hope without Optimism*. Yale. Yale University Press.
28 N. Timmins (1995). *The Five Giants: A Biography of the Welfare State*. London. Harper Collins.
29 The National Archives (1942). *Extract from Notes from the Advisory Panel on Home Affairs on Reconstruction Problems: The Five Giants on the Road, 25 June 1942 (T161/1165)*. Available at: www.nationalarchives.gov.uk/education/resources/attlees-britain/five-giants/. Last accessed July 2022.
30 P. Pietroni (2020). *The Poetry of Compassion*. Albuquerque. Fresco Books.
31 P. Pietroni (2020). *Compassion and the Other*. Albuquerque. Fresco Books.
32 W. Shakespeare (1603). *To Be, or Not to Be, That Is the Question*. Speech from Hamlet, spoken by Prince Hamlet, Nunnery Scene, Act 3, Scene 1. Available at: www.poetryfoundation.org/poems/56965/speech-to-be-or-not-to-be-that-is-the-question. Last accessed: March 2023.

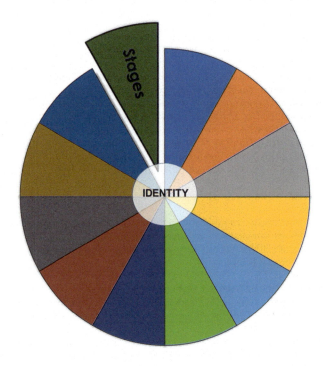

Figure 12.0

12 The Stages, the Seasons and the Life-Cycle of Man's Life

Figure 12.0

Introduction

Firstly, an apology. I recognise that inevitably I will be omitting much of the stages and life-cycle of a woman's life, but I will attempt to address this omission in Section 3 of this chapter.

In section 1: Biography, I will outline how I now see my own stages, seasons and life-cycle which will soon be overtaken by the end of my journey. I have been helped, guided, influenced by many: teachers; books I have read; friends I have had; wives I have married; holy men I have supped with; encounter groups I have attended, and more recently, poems I have both studied and written. I include three poems in this introduction which I will refer to from time to time.

In Section 2 I will attempt to cover and summarise some of the most important written material that has helped shape my thinking. The short list would include:

- The making and breaking of affectional bonds – *John Bowlby*[1]
- The making of maleness: men, women, and the flight of Daedalus – *Peter Tatham*[2]
- The human condition – *Hannah Arendt*[3]
- The hero with a thousand faces – *Joseph Campbell*[4]
- The hero within – *Carol S Pearson*[5]
- The chakras – *C W Leadbeater*[6]
- Choosing a path – *Sri Swami Rama*[7]
- The Tibetan book of the living and dying – *Sogyal Rinpoche*[8]
- On death and dying – *Elisabeth Kubler-Ross*[9]

I have already expanded on some of these texts in Chapter 10 (Psychology, Psychiatry, Psychoanalysis).

Finally, in Section 3 of this chapter I will tackle the concept of unconscious bias in an attempt to challenge "my story" as to its authenticity and truth.

DOI: 10.4324/9781003401414-13

170 *The Stages, the Seasons and the Life-Cycle of Man's Life*

All the world's a stage

All the world's a stage,
And all the men and women merely players;
They have their exits and their entrances;
And one man in his time plays many parts,
His acts being seven ages. At first the infant,
Mewling and puking in the nurse's arms;
And then the whining school-boy, with his satchel
And shining morning face, creeping like snail
Unwillingly to school. And then the lover,
Sighing like furnace, with a woeful ballad
Made to his mistress' eyebrow. Then a soldier,
Full of strange oaths, and bearded like the pard,
Jealous in honour, sudden and quick in quarrel,
Seeking the bubble reputation
Even in the cannon's mouth. And then the justice,
In fair round belly with good capon lin'd,
With eyes severe and beard of formal cut,
Full of wise saws and modern instances;
And so he plays his part. The sixth age shifts
Into the lean and slipper'd pantaloon,
With spectacles on nose and pouch on side;
His youthful hose, well sav'd, a world too wide
For his shrunk shank; and his big manly voice,
Turning again toward childish treble, pipes
And whistles in his sound. Last scene of all,
That ends this strange eventful history,
Is second childishness and mere oblivion;
Sans teeth, sans eyes, sans taste, sans everything.

William Shakespeare[10]

The Road Not Taken

Two roads diverged in a yellow wood,
And sorry I could not travel both
And be one traveler, long I stood
And looked down one as far as I could
To where it bent in the undergrowth;

Then took the other, as just as fair,
And having perhaps the better claim,
Because it was grassy and wanted wear;

The Stages, the Seasons and the Life-Cycle of Man's Life   171

Though as for that the passing there
Had worn them really about the same,

And both that morning equally lay
In leaves no step had trodden black.
Oh, I kept the first for another day!
Yet knowing how way leads on to way,
I doubted if I should ever come back.

I shall be telling this with a sigh
Somewhere ages and ages hence:
Two roads diverged in a wood, and I –
I took the one less traveled by,
And that has made all the difference.

Robert Frost[11]

The Listeners

'Is there anybody there?' said the Traveller,
Knocking on the moonlit door;
And his horse in the silence champed the grasses
Of the forest's ferny floor:
And a bird flew up out of the turret,
Above the Traveller's head:
And he smote upon the door again a second time;
'Is there anybody there?' he said.
But no one descended to the Traveller;
No head from the leaf-fringed sill
Leaned over and looked into his grey eyes,
Where he stood perplexed and still.
But only a host of phantom listeners
That dwelt in the lone house then
Stood listening in the quiet of the moonlight
To that voice from the world of men:
Stood thronging the faint moonbeams on the dark stair,
That goes down to the empty hall,
Hearkening in an air stirred and shaken
By the lonely Traveller's call.
And he felt in his heart their strangeness,
Their stillness answering his cry,
While his horse moved, cropping the dark turf,
'Neath the starred and leafy sky;
For he suddenly smote on the door, even

172 *The Stages, the Seasons and the Life-Cycle of Man's Life*

Louder, and lifted his head: –
'Tell them I came, and no one answered,
That I kept my word,' he said.
Never the least stir made the listeners,
Though every word he spake
Fell echoing through the shadowiness of the still house
From the one man left awake:
Ay, they heard his foot upon the stirrup,
And the sound of iron on stone,
And how the silence surged softly backward,
When the plunging hoofs were gone.

Walter de la Mare[12]

Section 1: Biography

I have chosen to identify and describe (using Shakespeare's "seven ages of man") what I consider the seven Russian dolls that exist somewhere in my psyche and have helped shape my identity through the years. I have already expanded on these in the chapter on psychology/psychoanalysis. These dolls will still emerge as both a conscious and, at times, on an unconscious level, influence my behaviour and my actions. Another metaphor I find helpful is to imagine them (the dolls) like the seven octaves of a piano. I, the pianist, can get stuck and "play out" in only one or two of these octaves, forgetting that my "piano" has many more. The psychologist, Edward Edinger, expands on this framework and labels it the ego-self axis (see Chapter 10). I find the images of the Russian dolls and the piano keyboard a very helpful reminder of how one's identity is forever in continuous flux i.e. I may be approaching my eighth decade, but I am still capable of acting as if I were still an infant or schoolboy of eight years old.

Section 2: Academic Literature Regarding Work

I will expand a little on the columns three and four which can only touch briefly on the extensive academic literature, novels, poems that expand on the "seven stages". I have chosen to focus on my reading as it impinges on the "seven Russian dolls" that I carry with me.

0–5 Years – Infant

John Bowlby and Donald Winnicott were two British psychologists who "strayed away" from the originators, Freud and Jung. They were both colleagues and also adversaries. Judith Issroff's book entitled with their names is an excellent account of their personal and professional perspectives. They both understood

The Stages, the Seasons and the Life-Cycle of Man's Life   173

Shakespeare's Seven Stages	My Seven Russian Dolls	Academic Sources	Focus
0–5 years "Infant"	Not breastfed Needy/greedy Uncontrolled rage	John Bowlby Donald Winnicott	Attachment theory "Good enough"
5–17 years "School Boy"	Competitive Controlling Bully	Jean Piaget Maurice Irfan Coles Elena Aguilar	Psychology of child Compassionate school CoED Foundation
17–30 years "Lover"	Co-dependant Narcissistic/charming Failed marriages	Marie-Louise von Franz Carol Pearson Nick Duffell	Puer Aeternus The hero within The making of them
30–60 years "Soldier"	Climbing the ladder Professional success Awards and prizes	Daniel Levinson Robert Bly Peter Tatham	Seasons of a man's life Iron John The making of MALENESS
60–75 years "Justice"	Spiritual search Cultural pursuits Opera and poetry 3-wise men, 3-wise women	Hannah Arendt Hermann Hesse Swami Rama	The Human Condition Journey to the East Choosing a Path
75–80 years "Slippered Pantaloon"	Introspection "found my voice" Chakras Stoic	Erik Erikson Edward Edinger Marcus Aurelius	Life history of the historical moment Ego and archetypes Chakras Meditation
80-? "Second Childishness"	Laughter, compassion My shed, my many sheds My legacy	Sogyal Rinpoche Kubler-Ross Patrick Pietroni	Tibetan Book of the Dead Death and Dying This Book

Figure 12.1 Shakespeare's Seven Stages and My Russian Dolls

and expanded on the statement, "*Give me the first five years of a child's life and I will give you a saint or a devil*".

Both Bowlby and Winnicott through meticulous research, as well as hours of clinical work, gave to us the concepts of "attachment behaviour" (Bowlby) and the "good enough mother" (Winnicott).

Bowlby began his life work before the Second World War. His first responsibility was working with young boys who were separated from their families for petty crimes. Bowlby's work differs in one central and crucial way from the work of many analytic theorists. It is not based solely on the retrospective formulation of clinical data but on observational data gathered in many different situations outside the analyst's room.

174   *The Stages, the Seasons and the Life-Cycle of Man's Life*

In brief, Bowlby argues:

> Attachment behaviour, it is argued, is a form of instinctive behaviour that develops in humans, as in other mammals, during infancy, and has as its aim or goal/proximity to a mother-figure. The function of attachment behaviour, it is suggested, is protection from predators. Whilst attachment behaviour is shown especially strongly during childhood when it is directed towards parent figures, it none the less continues to be active during adult life when it is usually directed towards some active and dominant figure, often a relative but sometimes an employer or some elder of the community.[13,14]

In summary, I would add that we now have the anthropological, the psychological (Bowlby), the biological (Lorenz) and the scientific (neuro imagining) evidence to support the view that:

a. The first five years of an infant's experience are of major importance in the learning he/she achieves.
b. This learning involves language and emotional/relational cognitive skills.
c. The "mother" or substitute mother is the critical input into what the child learns, especially in the emotional education between five and 17/18 years of age.

Donald Winnicott qualified as a doctor in 1920 and went onto specialise in paediatrics. He later also trained as a psychoanalyst and his major work and interest was working with children and their mothers. Like Bowlby, he is remembered for some pithy quotes: *"The foundation of the health are laid down by the ordinary mother in her ordinary loving care of her own baby"*.[15] There is much overlap between Bowlby and Winnicott, even though they were both critical of each other's work. Winnicott's phrase "the good enough mother", and "good enough parenting" have helped to make the psychoanalytic language both understandable and meaningful. Winnicott also emphasised the importance of play in creating a sense of being as opposed to "just" a sense of doing. His book, *Playing and Reality*,[16] couched in more formal psychoanalytic language, expanded on his other well-known concept of "true self" and "false self". He wrote, *"Only the true self can be creative and only the true self can feel real"*.[17]

For Winnicott, the true self allowed the child (and adult) to feel truly alive. To feel alive makes it possible to feel close to each other, and foster creativity. Both Bowlby and Winnicott broke away from the traditional psychoanalytic methodology of "the couch" and emphasised the importance of "playing and reality".

5–17 Years – School Boy

Jean Piaget, the Swiss psychologist (1896–1980), laid the groundwork for what was to become the major influencing factors in "experimental" educational

The Stages, the Seasons and the Life-Cycle of Man's Life   175

approaches. Piaget trained in philosophy and natural history before becoming a psychologist. He became interested in psychoanalysis and was appointed as Professor of Psychology, Philosophy and Sociology at the University of Neuchatel. He then was asked to become Director of the International Bureau of Education. Further invitations from French, Swiss and American universities were to follow.

Piaget's work on cognitive development helped to alter and shape many of the experimental American and European educational programmes e.g. Alexander Neil at Summer Hill School (1921, Suffolk, UK) and the Montessori Method founded by Dr Maria Montessori, the Italian paediatrician/psychiatrist. Piaget was quoted as saying,

> Education, for most people, means trying to lead the child to resemble the typical adult of his society . . . but for me and no one else, education means making creators. . . . You have to make inventors, innovators – not conformists.[18]

There are several similarities between these educational approaches embedded in the philosophy of these experiments – these included: "Freedom, not licence", "choice and self-direction" – a focus on collaboration and not competition. The combination of independent, small groups and whole group learning helps to stimulate collaboration, leadership and life-long learning.

It is only latterly that in my own teaching I now almost always introduce some poem. Poetry is of particular importance in our education system, both formal and informal.

> Compassion is one of the oldest, simplest and most intuitive forces in human history. It is a universal, timeless and radical concept that does not depend on any one culture. It can give our lives a sense of meaning and purpose, and contribute to our health and wellbeing. Although we are wired for compassion, our old brain psychologies – the cortisone-driven fear and flight mode – serve to undermine our better instinct. The best of world religions, the ancient contemplative traditions and contemporary secular neuroscience, psychology and mindfulness provide significant supportive signposts in our journey towards the compassionate school. Access for young people, however, depends on the context of their upbringing, whom they meet and what they read and watch. What is urgently required is an education system that teaches about compassion, teaches compassionately and encourages 'acts of love': a system, in short, that has collaboration and service as its highest ideals.
>
> On one level this looks like the agenda from hell – another series of impossible burdens that, once again, principals, teachers, support staff and governors are asked to shoulder with no extra resources and no overall direction. But, on another, it looks manageable. Yes, it is a big agenda but it is something schools are already doing in many ways. The trick is to begin to

176   *The Stages, the Seasons and the Life-Cycle of Man's Life*

make the compassionate journey intentional, to make it the key organizing principle of school life. It will, of course, need to be achieved on an incremental basis with each area of school life scrutinized through the prism of compassion.

Education and society's tectonic plates are shifting. They are moving away from a narrow attainment-based, individualistic, consumerist focus to something that stresses collaboration and service. Let us not, however, make our claims too extravagant. Compassion – and compassionate education – is not a magic want, a panacea for all the world's ills. No such thing exists. It can, however, be the magic wardrobe through which young people can walk to find their own solutions to the problematic legacies we are leaving behind.

Educators have a key role, if not the key role in helping to bring this about. This book has tried to provide a theoretical underpinning and practical supportive steps. But how do we know if we have achieved it? What would a compassionate school actually look like?[19]

17–30 Years – Lover

In discussing the concept of the "lover", I have found that Jung's theory of archetypes very helpful. For Jung, his theory of archetypes represented his most important theoretical contribution and hastened his break with Freud. For many analysts, even those well predisposed to Jungian ideas, archetypal formulations can have the feel of "high-faluting portentous language" that obfuscate rather than enhance discussion (Rycroft, 1982). Even within the Jungian field there is much debate as to their usefulness within clinical work. For example, Fordham, one of Jung's principal followers in London, is cautious regarding an analyst's tendency to relate personal imagery to myth, folklore or legend. Such a focus in Fordham's view can lead to the patient losing contact with his personal context of his unconscious material.[20]

Where archetypal formulations can help, however, to enhance debate is where they are linked to ethological concepts of human behaviour, especially when they draw on universal themes that transcend individual as well as cultural norms. Thus, archetypes can be described as "biological norms of psychic activity" that exert an influence on experience tending to organise it according to a pre-existing pattern.

Jung's theory of archetypes resembles Plato's notion of "Original Ideas", Bastian's concepts of "Elementary Ideas" and Schopenhaur's "Prototypes". Similar concepts can be identified in some Kleinian writers – Issac's "unconscious fantasy" and Bion's "preconceptions" being the closest.

The common thread which I wish to develop in relation to this particular section is that certain behaviour patterns seem to exist within the human species which are sufficiently common, occur significantly regularly, are environmentally stable and exert such a force on human growth that they act as a template for subsequent

The Stages, the Seasons and the Life-Cycle of Man's Life 177

experiences. Within clinical work, Jungians recognise a "hierarchy of archetypes" – the persona, the shadow, animus/anima and the self. Other archetypal motifs are to be found in a variety of literary and artistic forms. I have drawn upon the literature regarding "the Lover", more often identified as puer aeternus.

Marie-Louise von Franz, in her book "*Puer Aeternus*" defines this archetype as follows,

> In the practical life of the puer aeternus, that is, of the man who has not disentangled himself from the eternal youth archetype, one sees the same thing: a tendency to be believing and naive and idealistic, and therefore automatically to attract people who will deceive and cheat such a man. I have often noticed in analyzing men of that kind how they, in a fatal way, are attracted to rather dubious women or pick up friends about whom one does not have a good feeling. It is as though their inexperienced naiveté and their wrong kind of idealism automatically call forth the opposite, and it is no use warning such people against such relationships. You will only be suspected of jealousy, or something similar, and not listened to. Such naïveté or childish innocence can only be cured of these illusions by passing through disappointment and bad experiences. Warnings are no good – such men must learn by experience, without which they will never be awakened from their innocence. It is as if the wolves – namely, the crooks and destructive people – instinctively see such lambs as their legal prey. This naturally leads much deeper into the whole problem of our religious tradition.
>
> As you know, Christ is the shepherd and we are the sheep. This is a paramount image in our religious tradition and one which has created something very destructive, namely, that because Christ is the shepherd and we the sheep, we have been taught by the Church that we should not think or have our own opinions, but just believe. If we cannot believe in the resurrection of the body – such a mystery that nobody can understand it – then one must just accept it. Our whole religious tradition has worked in that direction.[21]

As Peter Tatham points out in "*The Makings of Maleness*",

> But for all of this, the Christian church overall has remained hostile to the Lover. The Lover has fared little better in Judaism. In Orthodox Judaism, the Lover, projected onto women, is still depreciated. The traditional Jewish prayer books still include, as part of the preliminary morning service, the sentence "Blessed art thou, Lord our God, King of the universe, who hast not made me a woman". And in Judaism, so the story goes, Eve was the one who first sinned. This slander against women, and by implication, against the Lover with whom she has been linked, sets the stage for the Jewish (and later the Christian and Moslem) notion of the woman as "seductress" who works to distract pious men from their pursuit of "holiness".

178   *The Stages, the Seasons and the Life-Cycle of Man's Life*

In Islam women have been notoriously depreciated and oppressed. Islam is a religion of Warrior energy asceticism. But even here the Lover has not been banished. The Moslem paradise after death is shown as Lover territory. Here all that the Moslem saint has forsworn and repressed in his earthy life is restored to him in the form of an endless banquet at which he is attended by beautiful women, "black-eyed houris".

Hinduism is different; it is not moralistic or ethical religion in the same sense that the Western religions are. Its spirituality is much more aesthetic and mystical. At the same time that Hinduism celebrates the Oneness of all things (in Braham) and the human oneness with God.[22]

Personally, I found reading both of these books liberating and an explanation of why my own adolescence and attempts at "loving" were so guilt-ridden, especially my regular masturbation.

But the puer aeternus, exemplified by von Franz, is the story of *"The Little Prince"*[23] by Antoine de Saint-Exupéry, has work to do. He has to differentiate with the different forms of love, eros, amor philos and agape. In Carl Kerényi's chapter, *The Primoridal Child in Primordial Times* in the book by Carl Jung and Carl Kerényi, *Essays on a Science of Mythology: The Myth of the Divine Child and the Mysteries of Eleusis*[24] Kerényi, outlines the challenge by quoting a fairy tale of the Black Forest Tatars:

Once upon a time, long ago
There lived an orphan boy,
Created of God
Created of Pajana.
Without food to eat,
Without clothes to wear:
So he lived.
No woman to marry him.
A fox came;
The fox said to the youth:
"How will you get to be a man?" he said.
And the boy said:
"I don't know myself
How I shall get to be man!"

Tatham, again,

The man under the influence of the Lover wants to touch and be touched. He wants to touch everything physically and emotionally, and he wants to be touched by everything. He recognizes no boundaries. He wants to live out the connectedness he feels with the world inside, in the context of his powerful

The Stages, the Seasons and the Life-Cycle of Man's Life 179

feelings, and outside, in the context of his relationships with other people. Ultimately, he wants to experience the world of sensual experience in its totality.[25]

Something I also resonate with, and as von Franz emphasises,

> However, there is another type of puer that does not display the charm of eternal youth, nor does the archetype of the divine youth shine through him. On the contrary, he lives in a continual sleepy daze, and that, too, is a typical adolescent characteristic: the sleepy, undisciplined, long-legged youth who merely hangs around, his mind wandering indiscriminately, so that sometimes one feels inclined to pour a bucket of cold water over his head. The sleepy daze is only an outer aspect, however, and if you can penetrate it, you will find that a lively fantasy life is being cherished within.[26]

30–60 Years – Soldier

"The Seasons of a Man's Life",[27] by Daniel J Levinson, is a masterly book that traces through detailed and long-term research in clear perspective on adulthood in men. It may appear that its limited focus does not allow for any generalised message to emerge. However, more than the descriptive and research findings, this detailed account laid the groundwork for others to follow. The terms life-cycle and life span, and the concept of life having seasons, have enabled our vocabulary to mirror our experiences. The research sample consisted of 40 men, in four different occupational sub-groups (hourly worker; executive; academic; writers), and all from diverse social backgrounds. The research focuses on three different stages/seasons of these 40 men.

1. The Novice Phase: the early adult transition. Entering the adult world and the age thirty transition (17–32 years).
2. The Settling-Down Period: building a second adult life structure (32–43 years).
3. The Mid-Life Transition: becoming one's own man (43–48 years).

These three stages do not quite match Shakespeare's formulation of the "Seven Ages of Man", and Levinson very helpfully acknowledges this and includes three other versions of the ages of man.

Three versions of "The Ages of Man"

"The Sayings of the Fathers" (from the Talmud)

  5   yeas is the age for reading (Scripture);
 10   for Misnah (the laws);
 13   for the Commandments (Bar Mitzvah, moral responsibility);

180   *The Stages, the Seasons and the Life-Cycle of Man's Life*

15   for Gemara (Talmudic discussions; abstract reasoning);
18   for Hupa (wedding canopy);
20   for seeking a livelihood (pursuing an occupation);
30   for attaining full strength ("Koah");
40   for understanding
50   for giving counsel;
60   for becoming an elder (wisdom, old age);
70   for white hair:
80   for Gevurah (new, special strength of age);
90   for being bent under the weight of the years
100   for being as if already dead and passed away from the world.

Confucius

The Master said, At 15 I set my heart learning.
At 30, I had planted my feet firm upon the ground.
At 40, I no longer suffered from perplexities.
At 50, I knew what were the biddings of heaven.
At 60, I heard them with docile ear.
At 70, I could follow the dictates of my own heart; for what I desired no longer
   overstepped the boundaries of right.

Solon

0–7   A boy at first is the man; unripe; then he casts his teeth; milk-teeth befitting the child he sheds in his seventh year.
7–14   Then to his seven years God adding another seven, signs of approaching manhood show in the bud.
14–21 Still, in the third of the sevens his limbs are growing; his chin touched with a fleecy down, the bloom of the cheek gone.
21–28 Now, in the fourth of the sevens ripen to greatest completeness the powers of the man, and his worth becomes plain to see.
28–35 In the fifth he bethinks him that this is the season for courting, bethinks him that son will preserve and continue his line.
35–42 Now in the sixth his mind, ever open to virtue, broadens, and never inspires him to profitless deeds.
42–56 Seven times seven, and eight; the tongue and the mind for fourteen years together are now at their best.
56–63 Still in the ninth is he able, but never so nimble in speech and in wit as he was in the days of his prime.
63–70 Who to the tenth has attained, and has lived to complete it, has come to the time to depart on the ebb-tide of Death. [27]

The Stages, the Seasons and the Life-Cycle of Man's Life   181

Poetry has constantly offered its own version of the challenges/transitions and inevitability of death. John Milton in "*Paradise Lost*" describes (amongst other things) the mid-life crisis:

Paradise Lost

Which way shall I fly
Infinite wrath and infinite despair?
Which way I fly is hell; myself am hell;
And in the lowest deep a lower deep,
Still threat'ning to devour me, opens wide,
To which the hell I suffer seems a heaven.

John Milton[28]

Rupert Brooke, who did die young, wrote *"The Soldier":*

The Soldier

If I should die, think only this of me:
That there's some corner of a foreign field
That is for ever England. There shall be
In that rich earth a richer dust concealed;
A dust whom England bore, shaped, made aware,
Gave, once, her flowers to love, her ways to roam;
A body of England's, breathing English air,
Washed by the rivers, blest by suns of home.
And think, this heart, all evil shed away,
A pulse in the eternal mind, no less

Gives somewhere back the thoughts by England given;
Her sights and sounds; dreams happy as her day;
And laughter, learnt of friends; and gentleness,
In hearts at peace, under an English heaven.

Rupert Brooke[29]

And my own favourite by Thomas Hardy, which I have asked to be read at my funeral:

Afterwards

When the Present has latched its postern behind my tremulous stay,
And the May month flaps its glad green leaves like wings,

182　*The Stages, the Seasons and the Life-Cycle of Man's Life*

Delicate-filmed as new-spun silk, will the neighbours say,
"He was a man who used to notice such things?'

If it be in the dusk when, like an eyelid's soundless blink,
The dewfall-hawk comes crossing the shades to alight
Upon the wind-warped upland thorn, a gazer may think,
"To him this must have been a familiar sight".

If I pass during some nocturnal blackness, mothy and warm,
When the hedgehog travels furtively over the lawn,
One may say, "He strove that such innocent creatures should
come to no harm,
But he could do little for them; and now he is gone".

If, when hearing that I have been stilled at last, they stand at
the door,
Watching the full-starred heavens that winter sees,
Will this thought rise on those who will meet my face no more,
"He was one who had an eye for such mysteries?"
And will any say when my bell of quittance is heard in the gloom,
And a crossing breeze cuts a pause in its outrollings,
Till they rise again, as they were a new bell's boom,
"He hears it not now, but used to notice such things?"

Thomas Hardy[30]

60–75 Years – Justice

Shakespeare wrote of this phase of a man's life,

And then the justice,
In fair round belly with good capon lin'd,
With eyes severe and beard of formal cut,
Full of wise saws and modern instances;
And so he plays his part.[31]

The Talmud says, *"For becoming an elder wisdom, old age";*[32] Confucius, *"I heard them with double ears";*[33] Solon, *"Has come to the time to depart on the ebb-tide of death";*[34] and Levinson, using the term, "late adulthood" writes,

At around 60, there is again the reality and the experience of bodily decline. As I've mentioned there is statistically a gradual decline starting at about 30 and continuing its inexorable course over the remaining years. A man does not suddenly become "old" at 50 or 60 or 80. In the fifties and sixties,

The Stages, the Seasons and the Life-Cycle of Man's Life 183

however, many mental and physical changes intensify his experience of his own aging and mortality. They remind him that he is moving from "middle age" to a later generation for which our culture has only the terrifying term "old age". No one of these changes happens to all men. Yet every man is likely to experience several and to be greatly affected by them.[35]

By 60 I had sat at the feet of my guru (Swami Rama) and read *The Journey to the East* (Hermann Hesse);[36] *The Castaneda Trilogy*;[37] *St John of the Cross*;[38] *The Dancing Wu Li Masters* (Gary Zukav).[39] However, I do believe my love of poetry and Gustav Mahler began to help shape my spiritual search in a direction I had not foreseen or understood.

I had also by then developed the habit of talking to my "three wise men" and "three wise women" (see Chapter 3). My work at the Himalayan Institute in my 30s and 40s allowed me to develop the discipline of meditation and pranayama (the yogic approach to breathing).

I have taken the liberty in this section to refer to some of my own writings on this subject, none of it is original and all of it is the product of my reading, studying and pursuing my own spiritual search. To quote from my book, "*The Greening of Medicine*",

Prayer and contemplation/relaxation and meditation

As outlined earlier, one of the ways in which 'spirit' has been interpreted is to separate it altogether from organised religion and a set of beliefs and link it to a 'special way of being'. Spirit and spiritual states are seen as something beyond the mundane and everyday. The notion of spirit is linked to the concept of life-force, a transcendent or mystical state of consciousness. It is this link to consciousness that has produced a reawakening of interest and study into matters spiritual. Like spirit, consciousness can be difficult to define but we can come nearer to studying and observing different states of consciousness through the use of electro-encephalograms and the measurement of brainwave activity. The very many disciplines that have been involved in the study of consciousness have all arrived at a different definition:

By consciousness I understand the relation of psychic contents to the ego in so far as this relation is perceived as such by the ego. Relations to the ego that are not perceived as such are not perceived as such are unconscious. Consciousness is the function or activity which maintains the relation of psychic contents to the ego.

Carl Jung

A fact without parallel which defies all explanation or description. Nevertheless if anyone speaks of consciousness we know immediately and from our most personal experience what is meant by it.

Sigmund Freud

184 *The Stages, the Seasons and the Life-Cycle of Man's Life*

Consciousness is the recognition of the fact that there is an inner being who knows what is real and who is in charge of the organism and what happens.

Philip Lee

Our normal waking consciousness, rational consciousness, as we call it, is but one special type of consciousness, whilst all about it, parted from it by the flimsiest of screens, there lie potential forms of consciousness, entirely different. No account of the universe in its totality can be final which leaves these other forms of consciousness quite disregarded.

William James

Consciousness is "that of which one is aware".

Psychologists

Ordinary consciousness is an exquisitely evolved personal construction – sensory systems select a small amount of input data, the brain modifies and gates this sensory input; higher level cortical selectivity filters on the basis of needs, preconceptions and "sets".

Robert Ornstein

Ordinary consciousness is an illusion.

Hindu text

According to which assumptions we make, the steam of consciousness is one of the following:

1. A complex of mental activities changing and flowing in time;
2. A succession of states, each real yet different in quality and kind from each other;
3. A personal participation in universal (cosmic) consciousness;
4. A flow of personal experience;
5. An epiphenomenal by-product of continuous brain functioning;
6. A matter of schedules of reinforcement provided by our social environment;
7. Subjective awareness correlated with brain functioning;
8. A set of emergent properties or characteristics.

J Strange[40]

Shakespeare has used the word "justice" to describe this stage in man's development. I have not been able to clarify for myself what he meant. Most philosophers from Plato to John Rawls[41] have attempted to explain its meaning; some employing the tenets of the Abrahamic religions, but the list of epithets that come before the word justice is very long e.g. social redistributive, reparative, relational, restorative – the list is long. I would hope he meant to imply that by the age of 60 we had learnt the meaning of all these forms of justice and we were committed to "doing justice".

I cannot leave this descriptive piece without mentioning Hannah Arendt; her two books: *Eichmann in Jerusalem: A Report on the Banality of Evil*[42] and *The Human Condition*[43] provide us with an understanding of the "shadow-side" of "justice". I have outlined some of her views in my book, *Morality, the Religions and the Poetry of Compassion* (2021).[44]

75–80 Years – Slippered Pantaloon

I write this section as I am about to have my 79th birthday, and it is to Erik Erikson that I turn to in his own psychosocial stages of life (I outline in greater detail in the chapter Psychology and Psychoanalysis). He labels this eighth stage, *ego integrity vs. despair*. It is also true that Shakespeare's "slippered pantaloon" describes how I potter around our home and my study. My slippers are only removed when I venture into my garden wearing boots. For Erikson, "wisdom" is defined as, "*informal and detached concerns for life itself in the face of death itself*". "Ego-integrity" means, "*the acceptance of life in its fullness; what you have accomplished and what you have not*". I would add my own aphorism, "*expect and accept*", and how, reading the stoic philosophers: Seneca, Zeno of Citium, Epictetus and especially Marcus Aurelius, has provided me with a daily guide and a framework for reflection and acceptance and Jung's theory of opposites and "living with the shadow".

One of the identities I now find I revel in is that of a grandfather. I have seven grandchildren and four that I have "adopted". In my early 50s and 60s I used to listen to Alistair Cooke's *Letter from America* and was mesmerised by the poetry that he was able to spin over the radio waves (well before Skype, Zoom or Facebook). Two years ago I started writing a letter from (whichever country I was then living in) once a month and sent it to all my grandchildren. Partly this arose out of my own memories of my own grandfather, once I became a grandfather myself. If you google "grandfather" and go past clock; mountain; paradox, there is little, if anything, to say about this "identity" which I now enjoy more than any other that I have allowed myself to own. I end with a poem,

I'll let you into a secret

I'll let you into a secret,
My grandfather
Made me laugh.
He sang to me in the car.
Taught me to swim,
And how to enjoy life.

186 *The Stages, the Seasons and the Life-Cycle of Man's Life*

I am now a grandfather
And am blessed
With many grandchildren.

They get on with their lives
And make sure I know
When their birthday is.
My one regret is
That I will not be
Alive to read their
Poems about me.
Nor was my grandfather.
I still think of him,
And that should be
Enough for me,
If they did too.
                    Patrick Pietroni[45]

80–? – Second Childishness

Shakespeare entitles this stage as "second childishness". I can personally vouch for this, as can my wife that I seem to laugh more these days, enjoy playing as if I were five years old (which can be extremely annoying and irritating to those around me). I have taken up new pursuits – growing a vegetable garden that is far too productive for two elderly adults to consume. I have built at least five (or is it six?) sheds from a potting shed to a wood shed, to a reading shed, and a workshop shed. They are in a way a containing wooden box in which I feel safe, contained and at peace with the world. Do I jump ahead, as I am prone to do, and do they represent the coffin in which I will not be buried in, as I will be cremated? I have made a "living will", spoken to all my children regarding my wishes, and settled my will. Most, if not all, of my close male friends have died (Bernard, Ronald, Brian, John). I am lucky to have remained good friends with my past wives, and also my first love from the age of 16. We communicate at birthdays and family gatherings and I do know that I can seek their advice or solace if I so need to. I have also written extensively on death and dying and will add that that my long period as a general practitioner gave me the privilege of looking after the dying patient and their grieving family. I like to quote this incident that occurred in our practice:

Dignifying Death

In the "*Tibetan Book of the Dead*",[46] which is a treatise on "how to die", it is considered that it is not possible to judge the value of a person's life until one

The Stages, the Seasons and the Life-Cycle of Man's Life   187

has witnessed his manner of dying. The Trukese, a Micronesian society, consider that the process of dying begins at forty. When a Trukese reaches the age of forty he can no longer climb trees as well as he used to, his strength begins to wane and when that happens he begins to prepare for his death.

Much of our own culture is geared not only to denying death but to retarding the ageing process. Science and medicine have lent themselves readily to this process. We have developed an impressive array of procedures, chemical agents, multivitamins, mineral preparations, and reconstructive surgical processes whose aim is to prolong life, often at the expense of the living. Once patients were removed from home so that they could die in hospital, we limited our contact as well as our children's with death. That is not to deny that hospitals and expert nursing do not play a valuable part in caring for the terminally ill patient. Indeed, it could be argued that more suffering occurred at home than in hospital and several surveys by the Marie Curie Foundation (1952)[47] and seem to suggest that romanticising the death bed scene at home is a real danger. Although traditional cultures may well have responded to death differently from us, psychologically death has always been a fearful and frightening experience.

Probably there is no greater factor which determines the nature of our healthcare system than our attitudes towards death. Much of medicine is organised and devoted to do battle with death. Doctors and nurses consider themselves to have failed if a patient dies. Studies amongst doctors have found them to be afraid of death in greater proportion than a control group of patients[48] and a time-and-motion study of a hospital ward indicated that doctors and nurses spent less time with the patients once they had identified that he or she is dying.[49] These attitudes coincide at a time when the percentage of people dying in hospital is continuing to increase. It is against this background that several remarkable pioneers began their work which has helped to influence not only are at a deuce towards the terminal ill but our approach to patient care in general.

Early Native American cultures in America would shoot arrows in the air to drive away the evil spirits associated with the dead. Firing guns at military funerals is not too dissimilar a ritual. Because of this fear of death and his inability to "know" the answers to the perennial question "is there life after death?", man has tended to deny the existence of this inevitable event and erect a complicated edifice of subterfuge and evasion which permeates the topic. Nevertheless, it is possible to trace certain consistent patterns of behaviour and forms of belief which are present in many different cultures. Rituals are seen as "rites of passage", the only accepted forms of behaviour which surround a naturally occurring human and social transition e.g. birth, marriage, death. In his examination of rituals surround death, Hertz[50] observed that two forms of death are commonly observed: biological and social death. Between these two events a period of time elapses which may be a few days to a year or indeed may be prolonged for ever. Biological death is the loss of physical identity – the person's body is

188 *The Stages, the Seasons and the Life-Cycle of Man's Life*

no longer present, and social death is the loss of the person's presence-influence and enables the family to continue living without him.

Socrates felt that philosophy – the love of wisdom – was "simply and solely the practice of dying – the practice of death", and to deny this meant that the individual was not a philosopher. Socrates' view of the body is very similar to that found in Eastern texts – a prison. Death provided the opportunity for the soul to travel to its rightful destination – God – and he felt each person had a guardian spirit which helped guide the soul once released back to Hades. This journey was difficult and had many "breaks and branches" and entailed the crossing of many rivers – Acheron – the river of pain, Pyriphlegthon – the river of burning.[51]

Judaism has three great tenets – free will, God and immortality – like how Socrates believes that death sets the soul free and permits it to depart the mortal life. When Rabbi Bunam was dying, his wife was weeping inconsolably by his side. "Why weep?" he said, "All my life has been given me merely that I might learn to die".[52]

Christianity teaches that the human soul is not naturally immortal. Only through Christ's resurrection and belief in that can the soul reach Heaven: "He that believeth hath eternal life". Unlike many Eastern religions, Christianity does not believe in destiny or fate. Through the act of forgiveness and atonement, Grace enters the human being and his journey to God is assured – body and soul. For many people, both Eastern and Western, the concepts of resurrection and reincarnation, although very different, provide the hope that dispels the fear of death. Death in all major religions has involved a meeting with the Gods, whether "natural" or "divine". Indeed, Greek doctors under the influence of Hippocrates believe it to be unethical to treat a patient who is in the grip of a "fatal illness", for to do so, the doctor pitted himself against nature and ran the risk of that fateful hubris that awaited those mortals who challenged the Gods. In *"The Indignity of "Death with Dignity"",*[53] Ramsay wrote there is a growing agreement amongst moralists that death has again to be accepted and all that can be done for the dying is to keep them company in their final moments.

At about the same time, Elizabeth Kubler-Ross began her multidisciplinary seminars on the care of the dying patient. Her point of departure was her perception that dying in hospital was lonely, mechanical and dehumanised. Following some major resistance from medical staff, she interviewed over 200 patients who were in the last stages of life. This was the first time that any systematic attempt had been made to obtain the views from patients of this inevitable consequence to terminal disease. Each interview was tape recorded and analysed. Kubler-Ross's five "Stages of Dying"[54] is now taught in many different clinical institutions. Although providing a structure for understanding why a patient may be behaving in a particular way, they can also be used as yet another checklist of questions, thus avoiding the human contact that will keep them company in their final moments. Nevertheless, Kubler-Ross's work has allowed for a greater

The Stages, the Seasons and the Life-Cycle of Man's Life   189

discussion to take place and has begun to break down the taboo surrounding death amongst healthcare workers.

The Five "Stages of Dying"

1. Denial – "No, not me". This is a typical reaction when a patient learns that he or she is terminally ill. Denial is important and necessary. It helps cushion the impact of the patient's awareness that death is inevitable.
2. Rage and anger – "Why me?" the patient resents the fact that others will remain healthy and alive while he or she must die. God is a special target for anger, since He is regarded as imposing, arbitrarily, the death sentence. To those who are shocked at her claim that such anger is not only permissible but inevitable, Dr Kubler-Ross replies succinctly, "God can take it".
3. Bargaining – "Yes, me, but . . .". Patients accept the fact of death but strike bargains for more time. Mostly they bargain with God – "even amongst people who never talked with God before". They promise to be good or to do something in exchange for another week or month or year of life. Notes Dr Kubler-Ross: "What they promise is totally irrelevant, because they don't keep their promises anyway".
4. Depression – "Yes, me." First, the person mourns past losses, things not done, wrongs committed. But then he or she enters a state of "preparatory grief", getting ready for the arrival of death. The patient grows quiet, doesn't want visitors. "When a dying patient doesn't want to see you any more", says Dr Kubler-Ross, "this is a sign he has finished his unfinished business with you, and it is a blessing. He can now let go peacefully."
5. Acceptance – "My time is very close now and it's all right." Dr Kubler-Ross describes this final stage as "not a happy stage, but neither is it unhappy. It's devoid of feelings but it's not resignation, it's really a victory."[55]

The Hospice Movement

The hospice movement grew out of a realisation by its pioneering founder, Dame Cicely Saunders, of the inadequacies and difficulties encountered by patients, their relatives, doctor and staff when caring for the terminally ill within NHS hospitals.

Under Christian influence, the care of the dying patient began to assume more than just medical care. St Luke's Hospice (1893) and St Joseph's Hospice (1905) were early examples of the modern-day equivalent and themselves were the continuation of medieval monastic medical orders and the deaconess hospitals of Europe. St Christopher's Hospice was founded in 1967 with the express intention of not only providing terminal care for the in-patients but developing an education and research centre to enable other practitioners to learn the principles of terminal care.

190   *The Stages, the Seasons and the Life-Cycle of Man's Life*

Dame Cicely's philosophy of terminal care has slowly evolved and its influence has had a far wider impact on the caring of patients in general. A nun in St Joseph's Hospice expressed one of the guidelines offered to all medical and nursing personnel: "Feelings are facts in this house".[56] The concept of "total pain" – physical, mental, social and spiritual – was introduced to widen people's horizons concerning the nature of the task required of the medical staff. It became clear that many doctors and nurses experienced difficulty in talking to dying patients. Few people seem to be able to talk to dying patients with ease. In hospital the culture is generally one of denial both amongst doctors and relatives.

Bereavement and Grief

At the same time as an understanding of the need of the dying patient developed, it became clear that the survivors required the help of the health-care professionals. Dying of a "broken heart" and "grief" was not an uncommon cause of death in the seventeenth and eighteenth centuries. More recent studies have indicated quite how at risk the survivors are.

Parkes' classic work amongst widows and widowers showed an increased mortality rate in the first six months following the death of their spouses. More recently this has been linked to changes within the immune system of the survivors. A further study showed an increased mortality in the first year of bereavement and concluded that the risk was present amongst other close relatives and not just the surviving spouses. The rate of divorce amongst parents of children dying of cancer is 80%. The preventative value of bereavement counselling to high-risk groups using the "key person" card developed at St Christopher's Hospice illustrates how sensitive and well-constructed research can aid in the appropriate use of the counselling services.[57]

Guides on the psychological reaction to the loss of a loved one have helped identify the various responses that are commonly found. Parkes describes a process of realisation which may go through different stages: a) shock, disbelief, denial, followed by b) an intense preoccupation and longing for the lost person, moving through c) a period of depression, dejection and hopelessness, with finally d) a period of acceptance and resolution.[58]

Chimamanda Ngozi Adichie, one of my favourite authors (*Half a yellow sun; Americanah*), has written a small booklet on grief (*Notes on Grief*)[59] following the death of her father.

I finish with her introduction,

From England, my brother set up the Zoom calls every Sunday, our boisterous lockdown ritual, two siblings joining from Lagos, three from the United States, and my parents, sometimes echoing and crackly, from Abba, our ancestral home town, in southeastern Nigeria. On June 7th, there was my father, only his forehead on the screen, as usual, because he never quite knew

The Stages, the Seasons and the Life-Cycle of Man's Life 191

how to hold his phone during video calls. "Move your phone a bit, Daddy," one of us would say. My father was teasing my brother Okey about a new nickname, then he was saying that he hadn't had dinner because they'd had a late lunch, then he was talking about the billionaire from the next town who wanted to claim our village's ancestral land. He felt a bit unwell, had been sleeping poorly, but we were not to worry. On June 8th, Okey went to Abba to see him and said that he looked tired. On June 9th, I kept our chat brief so that he could rest. He laughed quietly when I did my usual playful imitation of a relative. "Ka chi fo," he said. ("Good night.") His last words to me. On June 10th, he was gone. My brother Chuks called to tell me, and I came undone.[60]

Section 3: Linking Theory to Biography

Fig. 12.1 on page 173 gives an indication in column 4 (Focus) how I now perceive my own "seven stages" of a man's life.

The combination of an insecure attachment to a mother-figure and the close attention to me by my father encouraged both my neediness, as well as my competitive and controlling personality. The small passage printed in the school journal when I was five years old, *"When I grow up I want to be a solider – because I like fighting"* has all the hallmarks of a "Russian doll" existing in my body and psyche for many decades thereafter.

Competing with my elder brothers and bullying my younger brother continued well into my next two-four decades.

My phase as a "lover", husband and marriage partner, could not be described as a success and led to two divorces. I believe I compensated these personal challenges by "climbing the ladder of professional work" and achieving many awards and prizes. My psychoanalytic training helped me to achieve some awareness of my deficits. The regular practice of pranayama (breath training) and meditation began to modify the negative aspects of my behaviour. I found adopting the "three wise men" and "three wise women" model of "prayer", together with the building of "sheds", where I felt contained has given me the "secure base" that I had not felt in my early life.

Reading the Stoics have been my "bible", and much more laughter and joy are present and evident.

Arriving at my ninth decade allows me to enjoy my role and duties of being a grandfather. My death is soon to occur, but I feel ready to meet the challenges that this will bring.

Notes

1 J. Bowlby (2005. Originally published 1979). *The Making and Breaking of Affectional Bonds*. Abington. Routledge.

192   *The Stages, the Seasons and the Life-Cycle of Man's Life*

2 P. Tatham (1992). *The Making of Maleness: Men, Women, and the Flight of Daedalus*. London. Karnac Books.
3 H. Arendt (1998). *The Human Condition*. Chicago. University of Chicago Press.
4 J. Campbell (1968). *The Hero with a Thousand Faces*. Princeton. Princeton University Press.
5 C. S. Pearson (1989). *The Hero within*. San Francisco. Harper.
6 C. W. Leadbeater (1978. Originally published 1972). *The Chakras*. Ferntree Gully. Quest Books.
7 Sri Swami Rama (1983). *Choosing a Path*. Honesdale. Himalayan Institute Press.
8 S. Rinpoche (1992). *The Tibetan Book of the Living and Dying*. San Francisco. Harper.
9 E. Kubler-Ross (1969). *On Death and Dying*. New York. Macmillan Publishing.
10 W. Shakespeare (1996). *The Complete Works of William Shakespeare (Special Editions)*. Ware. Wordsworth Editions.
11 R. Frost (1916). The Road Not Taken. In *Mountain Interval*. New York. Henry Holt & Co.
12 W. De la Mare (2014. First published 1912). The Listeners. In *The Listeners and Other Poems*. Berlin. Naboo Press.
13 Anon (2022). *Love-Money and Us*.
14 Bowlby (2005. Originally published 1979). *Op. Cit.*
15 D. Winnicott (2005. Originally published 1971). *Playing and Reality*. Abington. Routledge.
16 Winnicott (2005. Originally published 1971). *Ibid.*
17 Winnicott (2005. Originally published 1971). *Ibid.*
18 J. Piaget & B. Inhelder (2000. Originally published 1969). *The Psychology of the Child*. New York. Basic Books.
19 M. I. Coles (Ed.) (2015). *Towards the Compassionate School: From Golden Rule to Golden Thread*. London. UCL Institute of Education Press.
20 M. Fordham (1978). *Jungian Psychotherapy: A Study in Analytical Psychology.* Abingdon. Routledge.
21 M. von Franz (1981. First published 1970). *Puer Aeternus*. Waltham Abbey. Sigo Press.
22 P. H. Tatham (1992). *The Makings of Maleness: Men, Women, and the Flight of Daedalus*. London. Society of Analytical Psychology.
23 A. de Saint-Exupéry (2019. First published 1943). *The Little Prince*. London Egmont.
24 C. G. Jung & K. Kerényi (1949). *Essays on a Science of Mythology: The Myth of the Divine Child and the Mysteries of Eleusis*. Princeton. Princeton University Press.
25 Tatham (1992). *Op. Cit.*
26 von Franz (1981. First published 1970). *Op. Cit.*
27 D. J. Levinson (1978). *The Seasons of a Man's Life*. New York. Ballantine Books.
28 J. Milton (2003. Originally published 1667). *Paradise Lost*. London. Penguin Classics.
29 R. Brooke (1914). *The Soldier*. Available at: www.poetryfoundation.org/poetrymagazine/poems/13076/the-soldier. Last accessed: June 2022.
30 T. Hardy (2015. First published 1917). Afterwards. In *Moments of Vision and Miscellaneous Verses*. Available at: www.gutenberg.org/files/3255/3255-h/3255-h.htm page257. Last accessed: June 2022.
31 Shakespeare (1996). *Op. Cit.*
32 Levinson (1978). *Op. Cit.*
33 Levinson (1978). *Ibid.*
34 Levinson (1978). *Ibid.*
35 Levinson (1978). *Ibid.*

The Stages, the Seasons and the Life-Cycle of Man's Life   193

36 H. Hesse (2003. First published 1932). *The Journey to the East*. New York. Picador.
37 C. Castaneda (1968). *The Castaneda Trilogy: A Yaqui Way of Knowledge*. London. Penguin Books.
38 A. Peers (Ed.). (1962). *St John of the Cross*. Mulgave. Images Publishing Group.
39 G. Zukav (1980. Originally published 1979). *The Dancing Wu Li Masters*. New York. Bantam Books.
40 P. Pietroni (1990). *The Greening of Medicine*. London. Gollancz.
41 J. Rawls (1971). *A Theory of Justice*. Cambridge. Belnap Press of Harvard University Press.
42 H. Arendt (2006. First published 1963). *Eichmann in Jerusalem: A Report on the Banality of Evil*. London. Penguin Classics.
43 H. Arendt (2018. Frist published 1958). *The Human Condition*. Chicago. University of Chicago Press.
44 P. Pietroni (2021). *Morality, the Religions and the Poetry of Compassion*. Albuquerque. Fresco Books.
45 Professor Pietroni (2021). *I'll Let You into a Secret*.
46 Rinpoche (1992). *Op. Cit.*
47 National Cancer Survey Committee of the Marie Curie Memorial & Queen's Institute of District Nurses (QIDN) (1952). *Report on a National Survey Concerning Patients with Cancer Nursed at Home*. Wellcome Collection. Available at: https:// wellcomecollection.org/works/tcqmejmd. Last accessed: June 2022.
48 National Cancer Survey Committee of the Marie Curie Memorial & Queen's Institute of District Nurses (QIDN) (1952). *Ibid.*
49 National Cancer Survey Committee of the Marie Curie Memorial & Queen's Institute of District Nurses (QIDN) (1952). *Ibid.*
50 R. Hertz (1960). *Death and the Right Hand*. Abingdon. Routledge.
51 W. H. D. Rouse, M. S. Santirocco, & R. N. Goldstein (2015). *Great Dialogues of Plato: Complete Texts of the Republic, the Apology, Crito Phaedo, Ion, Meno, Symposium*. London. Signet.
52 Rouse, Santirocco, & Goldstein (2015). *Ibid.*
53 P. Ramsey (1974). The Indignity of "Death with Dignity". *The Hastings Center Studies* 2(2). pp. 47–62. Available at: www.jstor.org/stable/3527482. Last accessed: June 2022.
54 Kubler-Ross (1969). *Op. Cit.*
55 Kubler-Ross (1969). *Ibid.*
56 C. M. Saunders (Ed.) (1984). The Management of Terminal Disease. In *The Management of Terminal Malignant Disease*. Dunmore. Arnold Publishing.
57 C. M. Parkes (1975. Originally published 1972). *Bereavement; Studies of Grief in Adult Life*. London. Penguin.
58 C. M. Parkes (1981). Evaluation of a Bereavement Service. *Journal of Preventive Psychiatry* 1(2). pp. 179–188.
59 C. N. Adichie (2021). *Notes on Grief*. London. Fourth Estate.
60 Adichie (2021). *Ibid.*

Index

abortion 121
academic appointments 95–97
active imagination 68
Adichie, Ngozi 190–191
Adler, Alfred 26
Afghanistan debacle 152–153
Agarwal, Pragya 133
"Ages of Man, The" 179–180
Aguilar, Elena 77
All the world's a stage (Shakespeare) 170
alternative therapies 64
American Association of Physical
    Anthropologists 13
Anarchism 159
Antoine de Saint-Exupéry, 178
Antoninus Pius 156
Arendt, Hannah 44, 169, 185
Aristotle 139, 140, 155–156
Armenian Church 33
Armstrong, Karen 37
army experience 87–90, 179
artificial intelligence (AI) 153
Ascent of Money, The (Ferguson)
    127–128
associate professor 94–95
As You Like It (Shakespeare) 71
athletic pursuits 63
attachment theory 78, 81–82, 135,
    147, 191
attunement 79
Augustine of Hippo, Saint 156

Babushka dolls 1–2, 148
Bach, Johann Sebastian 62
Bader, Douglas 62
Balint, Michael 95, 136, 137
Barker, Ronnie 15

Barry, S. 136
beards 62
Behave (Sapolsky) 37
behavioural psychologists 143
belief 39
Benn, Tony 151
Bentham, Jeremy 158
bereavement 190–191
Beridze, Irakli 153
Beveridge Report 163
Biden, Joe 120
biography: body 61–64, 68–69; caste
    16; culture 116–118, 120–121;
    education 71–77, 82–82;
    ethnicity 15–16; family 19–23,
    29–30; gender 47–49, 57–58;
    life cycle 172–186, 191; money
    123–126, 130; national identity
    5–11; politics 151–154; race
    16; religion 33–37, 39–44; tribe
    16; work/professional positions
    85–101, 107–111
biology 50–51
Bion, W. 176
birth order theory 26, 29–30
Blair, Tony 102, 109–110, 151, 160
Blighton, Enid 72
Blumenbach, J. F. 13
body: biography 61–64, 68–69;
    languages 64–68
body-build 67
body-type 63
Bowlby, John 55, 78, 79, 147, 169,
    172–174
brain 145–147
Breuer, Josef 141
British Colonial culture 5, 8–10, 74

Index 195

British Medical Association (BMA) 64
Brooke, Rupert 181
Brooks, Peter 7
brother 20, 29–30
Brown, Gordon 151
Brown, N. 67
Bryan, Elizabeth 99
Buddhism 39, 40, 42
Bulmer, Martin 12, 13
Burke, Edmund 158
Byrne, P. S. 136

Callaghan, James 151
Cameron, David 151
Campbell, Joseph 169
Capitalism 159
Carter, Jimmy 36
Casey, Edward S. 116
Castaneda Trilogy (Castaneda) 183
caste 14–15, 16
Caste (Wilkerson) 15
Centre for the Psychological Studies 107
change management 105
Charles, Prince of Wales 130
"*Chimes, The* " (Dickens) 161
Christianity 39, 40, 42, 188
Christmas Carol, A (Dickens) 71
Cicero 118, 120, 156
citizenship 11
City of God (Augustine) 156
class 15, 15
Cleese, John 15
climate change 152
Clinton, Hillary 120
closed family 24
clothing 63–64
Coles, Maurice Irfan 79
Communism 159
compassionate school 79–80
Confucianism 40
Confucius 180, 182
conscious 141
consciousness 184–185
Conservatism 160–162
Constantine 156
Controlling Health Professionals
     (Harrison and Pollitt) 102
Cooke, Alistair 185
Copernicus 157
Corbett, Ronnie 15
Council of the European Union 13
cousin 22–23, 31

Covid 153
cradle to grave 108
creative destruction 129
Crisis of Confidence in Professional
     Knowledge, The (Schon) 101
Crisis of Professional Knowledge and
     the Pursuit of an Epistemology of
     Practice, The (Schon) 102
Crompton, Richmal 72
cultural studies 118–119
culture: academic studies 118–119;
     biography 116–118, 120–121;
     definitions 115–116
culture wars 1, 119–120
Cyprus: brief historical background 5–7;
     communities 6; Greek Cypriot
     Independence struggle 73;
     population 6; religion 33–35

Dancing Wu Li Masters, The (Zukav) 183
Darwin, Charles 62, 67
death: dignifying 186–191; hospice
     movement 189–190; stages of
     dying 189
Deconstructing Gender and Parallel
     Processes (Hakeem) 55
de la Mare, Walter 74, 171–172
Delusions of Gender (Fine) 50
Democratic Socialism 159
Descartes, René 140, 158
Dickens, Charles 161
Dictionary of Philosophy (Flew) 39
disease 163
divorce 21, 28–29, 48, 125
Doctor, his patient and the illness, The
     (Balint) 95, 136
dolls house family 29
Dooris, Mark 106
Douglas- Home, Alec 151
Dragons of Eden, The (Sagan) 147

early childhood 172–174
education: biography 71–77, 81–82;
     experimental approaches
     175–176; junior school 71–73;
     medical school 75–77, 103–105;
     preschool 71; psychological
     education 136–138; secondary
     school 73–75; training 77–81;
     university education 103–105
EFTP 133, 134
ego 142

Index

Eichmann in Jerusalem (Arendt) 185
electroencephalograph (EEG) 145
Elizabeth Bryan Foundation Trust 99
empathetic responses 78
empty nest syndrome 26
energy medicine 68
Enigmas of Identity, The (Brooks) 7
Enlightenment 153–154
Epictetus 148, 185
Eriksen, Thomas 12
Erikson, Erik 185
Essays on a Science of Mythology (Jung and Kerényi) 178
ethnic 13
ethnicity 12, 15–16, 153
evolution 7–8
Expression of the Emotions in Man and Animals, The (Darwin) 67

families: closed family 24; dolls house family 29; family dynamics 26; family relationships 26; groups 23–24, 29; illness 27–28; life cycle 25–26; marital conflict 28–29, 48, 125; open family 24–25; of origin 25; random family 24; scapegoating 29; types 23–29
family medicine 91–95
Famous Five, The (Blighton) 72
father 21, 30
feminine 52, 66
Ferguson, Niall 127–128
Fine, Cordelia 50–51
Five Giants, The (Timmins) 163
food 63–64
Foot, Michael 151
fragile masculinity 57, 58
Freeling, P. 136
Freud, Sigmund 7, 26, 37, 53, 76, 141–143, 172, 176, 183
friends 23, 31
friendship 23, 31
Frost, David 15
Frost Report (television show) 15
Frost, Robert 170–171

Galen 67
Galileo 157–158
Gandhi, Mahatma 44
gender: attributes 51–52; biography 47–49, 57–58; biology 50–51;

deconstruction 55; feminine 52, 66; identity 52, 53; masculine 52; role 51–52; toxic masculinity 55–57, 58, 154
general practice career 90
George Lucas Educational Foundation 77
Giving the Body its Due (Greene) 68
Golden Rule 39–41, 44, 80
Golden Thread 80, 81
Goodwin, Barbara 159
Graeber, David 41
grandfather 22, 31
grandson 22, 30
Great Britain 5–6
Greek Orthodox Church 22, 33, 34
Greene, Anita 68
grief 190–191
Griffiths, Roy 109
groups 23–24
Guevara, Che 62

Hadrian 156
hair 61–62
Hakeem, Az 55
Hall, E. T. 67
Hardy, Thomas 181–182
Harrison, S. 101
Healthy Universities (Dooris) 106
Heath, Edward 151
height 61
"Heroic Leadership is a Campus Villain" (Thomas) 105
Hertz, R. 186
Hesse, Hermann 183
Himmelfarb, Gertrude 154
Hinduism 39, 40, 178
Hippocrates 66, 67, 68, 140
Hobbes, Thomas 158
Holmes, Jeremy 44
Holmes, Sherlock 62
homosexuality 49
hospice movement 189–190
hospital doctor experience 86–87
Human Condition, The (Arendt) 185
humanistic psychologists 144–145
Hunter, John 68
husband 21, 30

id 144
idleness 164
Ignatus of Loyola 78
ignorance 1, 163–164

Index 197

illness 27–28
Indignity of "Death with Dignity" The
(Ramsay) 188
INFP 133, 134
instrumental perenialism 12
interpenetrating mix-up 137
IQ scores 134–135
Islam 39, 40, 178
I spend therefore I am (Roscoe) 129
Issroff, Judith 172

Jainism 40
James, William 184
job titles 85–86
Johnson, Boris 151
Journey to the East, The (Hesse) 183
Judaism 39, 40, 42, 177
Jukes, Adam E. 56
Jung, Carl G. 26, 37, 54, 55, 68, 138, 143,
172, 176, 178, 183
junior school 71–73
justice 182, 184
Just William (Crompton) 72

Keirsey, David 133
Kerényi, Carl 178
Key Variables in Social Investigation
(Burgess) 12
Klein, Melanie 54
Kolakowski, Leszek 37
Kretschmer, E. 67
Kristeva, Julia 55
Kubler-Ross, Elisabeth 169, 188–189

late adulthood 182–185
Latins 6, 33–34
Leadbeater, C. W. 169
leadership 105, 106
Lee, Philip 184
Leonardo Da Vinci 140
Letter from America (Cooke) 185
Levantine 16
Levelers 159
Levinson, Daniel J. 179, 182–183
Liberalism 157–158, 159
life cycle: biography 172–186, 191;
families 25–26; work/professional
positions 172–186
Listeners, The (de la Mare) 171–172
Little Prince, The (Saint-Exupéry) 178
Locke, John 158
London Teacher's Workshop 136

Long, B. E. L. 136
Lorenz, Karl 79, 174
lover 176–179

Machairas, Leontios 33–34
Machiavelli, Niccolò 156
MacLean, Paul 147
Macmillan, Harold 151
magnetic resonance imagining (MRI) 146
Mahler, Gustav 183
Major, John 102, 151
Makings of Maleness, The (Tatham) 177
Marcus Aurelius 148, 156, 185
Marie Curie Foundation 186
Marinker, M. 136
marital conflict 28–29, 48
market forces 109
Maronite Church 33
Marxism 159
Marylebone Health Centre. 130
masculinity 52, 55–57, 154
masturbation 48
Matryoshka dolls 1–2
May, Theresa 151
McCabe, Herbert 103
medical school 75–77, 103–105
meditation 43, 184
Mendel, Gregor 68
mentoring: definition 99; exemplar 100;
principles 99; programme 99;
programme outline 100
Milton, John 120, 181
mirror neurons 79–81
money: biography 123–126, 130; poetry
126–127; status 130; wealth
128–129
Montaigne, Michel de 158
Montessori, Maria 175
Montessori Method 175
Muslims 33
Myers Briggs Type Indicator (MBTI) 133

National Institute of Clinical Excellence
(NICE) 102
nationality 11–12
Native Americans 186
Natural Varieties of Mankind, On the
(Blumenbach) 13
Neil, Alexander 175
Nemesius 66
nephew 22–23, 31
Nerva 156

198 *Index*

neuroanatomy 140
neuroimaging 146–147, 174
neuroscience 146–147
neurosexism 50–51
new practice 91
Newton, Isaac 140, 158
NHS Bill 111

obesity 63–64
open family 24–25
Orbach, Susie 55
Ornstein, Robert 184
otherness 6–7
Outsider, The (Wilson) 24

Paradise Lost (Milton) 181
Parkes, C. M. 190
Patient Charter 110
Pavlov, Ivan 143, 144
Pearson, Carol S. 169
penis envy 48, 57
perpetual perenialism 12
personal identity 15–16
Physique and Character (Kretschmer) 67
Piaget, Jean 174–175
Pietroni, Anthony 34
pipe smoking 62
Plato 120, 139, 155–156, 176, 184
poetry 77, 175–176, 181–182
Poetry of Compassion Book Series 100
Political Liberalism (Rawls) 158
politics: biography 151–154;
        Conservatism 160–162; Greek
        originators 155–156; political
        theory 155–162; Socialism
        159–160
Pollitt, C. 102
prayer 184
preconscious 141
preschool 71
primary care trusts 111
Prince, The Machiavelli 156
private healthcare companies 111
Proust, Marcel 7
proxemics behaviour 67
psychiatrists 145–146
psychoanalysis 53–55, 141–143
psychoanalytic training 138–139
psychological education 136–139
psychology: behavioural psychologists
        143; biography 133–139;
        humanistic psychologists

144–145; psychological education
        136–138
Puer Aeternus (von Franz) 177

race 12–14, 15, 16, 153
Race and Ethnicity (Bulmer) 12, 13
racial 12–14
racial essentialism 13
racial groupings 13
Rajasekharan, Ramachandran 129
Rakel, David 26
Rakel, Robert 26
Rama, Sri Swami 169
Ramsay, P. 188
random family 24
Raphael 139
Rawls, John 158, 184
regulators 109–110
religion: biography 33–37, 39–44;
        Cyprus 33–34; divorce 28;
        masturbation 48; religion 42–44;
        spirit 41–42; types 39, 40–41;
        wise guides 44; wise words 44
Religion and the Rebel (Wilson) 24
Religion (Kolakowski) 37
Republic, The (Plato) 155
retirement/return to work 98–99
Rinpoche, Sogyal 169
Road Not Taken, The (Frost) 170–171
"Roads to Modernity, The"
        (Himmelfarb) 154
Rolf, Ida 66
Roman Catholic Church 5, 6, 19, 22, 29,
        33–34, 36, 48, 49, 78, 159
Roscoe, Philip 129
Rousseau, Jean-Jacques 7, 158
Rumi 44
Russell, Bertrand 62

Sagan, Carl 147
Saint Christopher's Hospice 189
Saint-Exupéry, Antoine de 178
Saint. John of the Cross (Peers) 183
Saint Joseph's Hospice 189–190
Saint Luke's Hospice 189
Salmon report 108
Sapolsky, Robert 37
Saunders, Cicely 189–190
scapegoating 29
Schon, Donald 101–103, 104, 154
school boy 174–176
"School of Athens, The" (Raphael) 139

Schopenhauer, Arthur 176
secondary school 73–75
second childishness 186
Seebohm report 108
Seneca 148, 185
senior level leaders 106–107
sexism 50
sexual difference 26
Shakespeare, William 67, 71, 120, 165–166, 170, 182, 184, 185
Sheldon, W. H. 67
Sikhism 40
situation perenialism 12
Skinner, B. F. 143, 144
slippered pantaloon 185
Smith, John 137
Socialism 159–160
Social Studies (Tavris) 50
Socrates 155–156, 188
"Soldier, The" (Brooke) 181
Solon 180
solo practice 91
son 20–21, 30
Southerton, Emily 78
spirit 41–42, 184
spiritual practice 42–44
sports 63
squalor 164
Starnge, J. 184
status 130
Stevenson, Malcolm 6
steward 106
stewardship 105, 106
strength 63
subtle-body 68
Summer Hill School 175
super-ego 144
Sway(Agarwal) 133
Swift, Richard 41

Talmud 179–180, 182
Taoism 40
Tatham, Peter 169, 177–179
Tavistock Clinic 36, 49, 78, 94, 138, 139
Tavris, Carol 50
teeth 62
temperaments 133
Textbook of Family Medicine (Rakel and Rakel) 26
Thatcher, Margaret 101, 108–109
Thomas, Mike 105
Thunberg, Greta 44

Tibetan Book of the Dead 186
Timmins, Nicholas 163
touch 64, 67
toxic masculinity 55–57, 58, 154
training 77–81
Trajan 156
Traveller, The (de la Mare) 74
tribalism 14
tribes 1, 14, 16
Trump, Donald 119, 120, 151, 153

unconscious 141
unconscious bias 1, 133, 169
Universal Declaration of Human Rights 11
university education 103–105
Using Political Ideas (Goodwin) 159

Vickers, Geoffrey 103, 104, 154
vital force 68
Voltaire 78, 158
von Franz, Marie-Louise 177, 179
voting rights 153

Wall, Nicholas 28–29
want 163
wealth 128–129
Weber, Max 12
Weizenbaum, Joseph 153
Wilkerson, Isabel 14
Wilson, Colin 24
Wilson, Harold 62, 151
Winnicott, Donald 172–173, 174
wise guides 44
wise words 44
Wollstonecroft, Mary 44
Wordsworth, William 42–43
work/professional positions: academic appointments 95–97; army experience 87–90; associate professor 94–95; biography 85–101, 107–111; family medicine 91–95; general practice career 90; hospital doctor experience 86–87; job titles 85–86; life cycle 172–186; medicine/healthcare service 101–103; new practice 91; retirement/return to work 98–99; solo practice 91

Zeno 148, 185
Zoroastrianism 40
Zukav, Gary 183

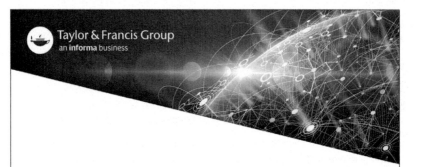